How To Use Chinese Abacus

A step-by-step guide to addition, subtraction, multiplication, division, roots and more ii

How To Use A Chinese Abacus

A step-by-step guide to addition, subtraction, multiplication, division, roots and more

Author:
Paul Green

First published 2007

Publisher: LULU
             Morrisville
             NC 27560
             USA

             http://www.lulu.com/content/1018833

ISBN: 978 1 84799 864 4

Preface

The Chinese abacus has been used as a calculation tool for generations and can still be seen in use in China today. Children are still taught to use this instrument in Chinese schools. It is widely available, cheap to buy and fun to use.

This book will teach you the skills needed to use an abacus proficiently, once learnt and practised these skills will stay with you for life. A useful and impressive skill that would be an asset for anyone.

Contents

PART 1

INTRODUCTION

Introduction 1

The Chinese abacus is called the Suan Pan (in Chinese 算盤) and in the form we know it today has a two bead and five bead combination. It appeared in approximately 1200 AD and has been used as a calculation tool for generations.

It is most commonly used for performing addition, subtraction, multiplication, division, square root and cube root calculations. With practice these calculations can be done with great speed.

Learning how to use the abacus can help to improve concentration, memory power and allow you to perform faster and more accurate mental arithmetic. It is also fun to learn and use.

The Chinese abacus consists of a wooden frame with a horizontal beam, wooden rods (usually 9 or 13 sometimes more) and seven hard wood beads on each rod, two beads above the beam and five beads below it.

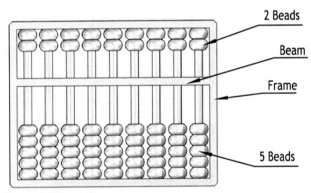

Figure 1.1 Chinese abacus

The Japanese abacus differs from the Chinese abacus by only having five beads on each rod, 1 bead above the beam and four beads below it.

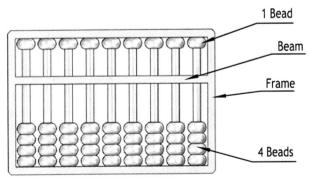

Figure 1.2 Japanese abacus

With the Chinese abacus it is possible to perform hexadecimal (base-16) and decimal (base-10) calculations. Today the decimal system is the most widely used and is the one that is followed in this book.

The decimal system is based on positioning digits in their places. The value of each place is ten times larger than the value of a place on its right.

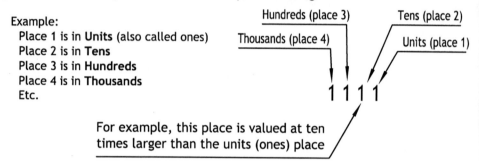

Example:
Place 1 is in **Units** (also called ones)
Place 2 is in **Tens**
Place 3 is in **Hundreds**
Place 4 is in **Thousands**
Etc.

Hundreds (place 3) Tens (place 2)
Thousands (place 4) Units (place 1)

1 1 1 1

For example, this place is valued at ten times larger than the units (ones) place

In modern abacus techniques, the use of the beads that touch the frame (base beads) are rarely used. When using the abacus with the decimal system it is not necessary to use them. Some older Chinese techniques use these base beads during calculations, these methods known as the 'Suspended bead technique' and the 'Extra bead technique' are explained in part 7 of this book.

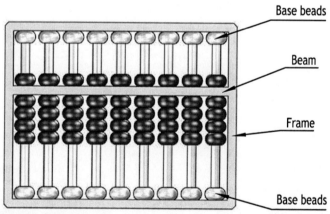

Base beads

Beam

Frame

Base beads

Figure 1.3 Chinese abacus

Common Chinese abaci have nine rods for the compact abacus and 13 rods for the normal size abacus (usually 200mm high). Other abaci with more rods, 17, 21, 23 and even 31 rods can be found and are very useful for performing more complicated calculations like square and cube roots.

PART 2
ABACUS PARTS

Abacus parts   2

The parts of a typical Chinese abacus

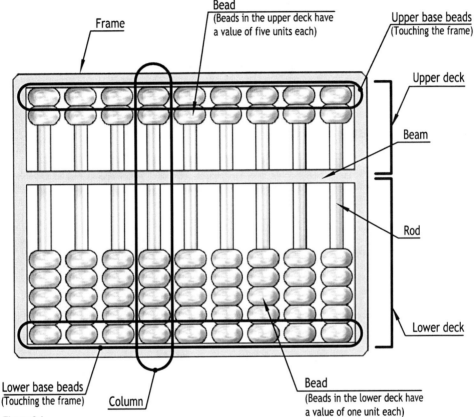

Bead
(Beads in the upper deck have a value of five units each)

Frame

Upper base beads
(Touching the frame)

Upper deck

Beam

Rod

Lower deck

Lower base beads
(Touching the frame)

Column

Bead
(Beads in the lower deck have a value of one unit each)

Figure 2.1

- **Beads** - Circular discs stacked on the rods.
  The part of the abacus that is used for the calculation.
  The beads are registered by moving them towards the beam, they are unregistered by moving the beads away from the beam.
  There are two beads in each upper deck part of a column and each bead has a value of five units.
  There are five beads in each lower deck part of a column and each bead has a value of one unit.
  The upper or lower base beads should not be moved from their position unless you are using the 'extra bead' method or the 'suspended bead' method (see part 7).

- **Beam** - The place where the beads are pushed against. The beads can then be used in the calculation (registered).

8

- **Column** - One column consists of one rod with seven beads stacked on it. There are nine columns in the compact abacus and thirteen in the normal sized abacus. Larger abaci with 17, 21, 23 and 31 rods are also available.

- **Frame** - Surrounds the abacus and supports the columns.

- **Lower deck** - The area below the beam.

- **Rod** - A circular rod where the beads are stacked and moved.

- **Upper deck** - The area above the beam.

The values of each column

The abacus columns each have a different value, known as counting in base 10. For example, starting from the right side of the abacus, the first column represents units in ones, the next column on the left represents units in tens, the next left column is units in hundreds etc..

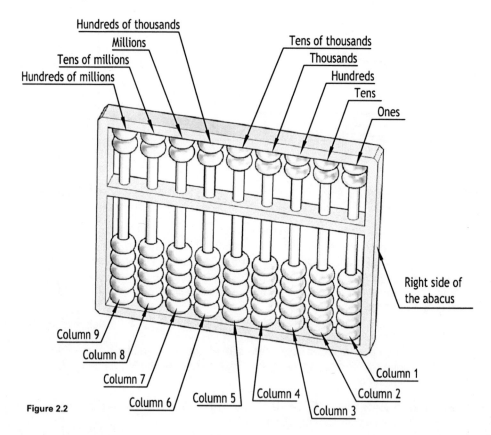

Figure 2.2

Registering numbers on the abacus

Registering is when you move a bead so that it is to be included in the calculation. When you move a bead so that it touches the beam, then this bead is said to be registered. When you move a bead away from the beam this is said to be **unregistered**, meaning that it will no longer be counted in the calculation. Throughout the book the computer terms '**Register**' and '**Unregister**' will be used to refer to beads that are moved towards the beam (register a bead) or away from the beam (unregister a bead).

The **Abacus result** can be obtained by reading the beads that are touching the beam (see figure 2.4).

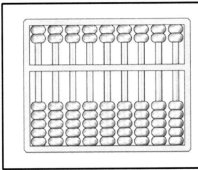

- No beads have been moved from their basic position

- The abacus result is 0

Figure 2.3

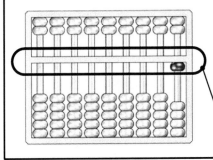

- One bead (from the lower deck which has a value of one unit) has been moved towards the beam (registered)

- The abacus result is 1

Abacus result
(Read all beads that are touching the beam)

Figure 2.4

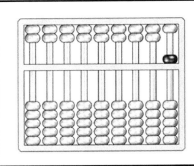

- One bead (from the upper deck which has a value of five units) has been registered

- The abacus result is 5

Figure 2.5

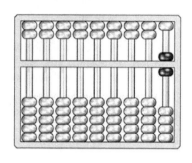

- One bead (from the upper deck which has a value of five units) has been registered

- One bead (from the lower deck which has a value of one unit) has been registered

- The abacus result is 5+1 = **6**

Figure 2.6

Registering numbers with more than one digit

When registering numbers with more than one digit i.e. 150, always start from the right side of the frame. For example, the number 150 has three digits so the first three columns on the right side of the frame are to be used, see example 2.9.

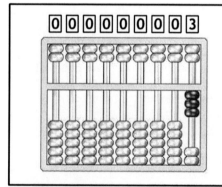

- Three beads from the lower deck have been registered in the first column

- The abacus result is **3**

Figure 2.7

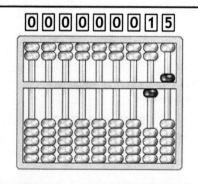

- One bead from the lower deck has been registered in the second column

- One bead from the upper deck has been registered in the first column

- The abacus result is **15**

Figure 2.8

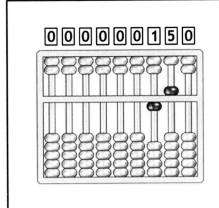

- One bead from the lower deck has been registered in the third column

- One bead from the upper deck has been registered in the second column

- No beads have been registered in the first column

- The abacus result is **150**

Figure 2.9

Some example numbers on the abacus

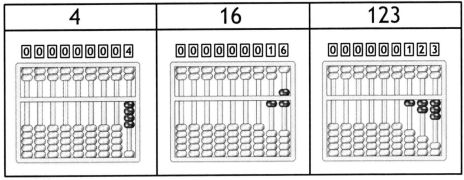

| 4 | 16 | 123 |

Figure 2.10

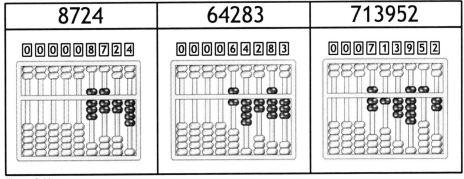

| 8724 | 64283 | 713952 |

Figure 2.11

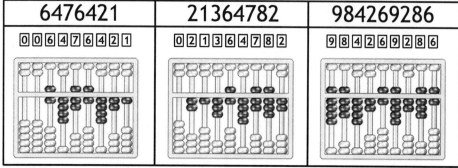

6476421	21364782	984269286
006476421	021364782	984269286

Figure 2.12

What figures are shown on the abacus?
(see page 135 for the answers)

Question	
1	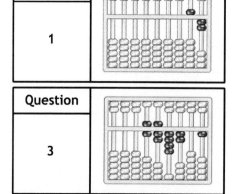

Question	
2	

Question	
3	

Question	
4	

Register the following figures on your abacus
(see page 135 for the answers)

Question	Register this figure
5	7
6	12
7	18
8	432
9	1208
10	23456
11	556677
12	482014365

PART 3

ADDITION

Addition 3

Addition is adding numbers to get the sum of those numbers.

When performing addition on the abacus:
- The numbers are registered on the abacus from the left side to the right side.
- Each digit must be entered in the correct column.
  For example, when adding two numbers that have three digits each, start by registering the first number in the first three columns then make the addition of the second number, again in the first three columns.

Example: 231 + 213

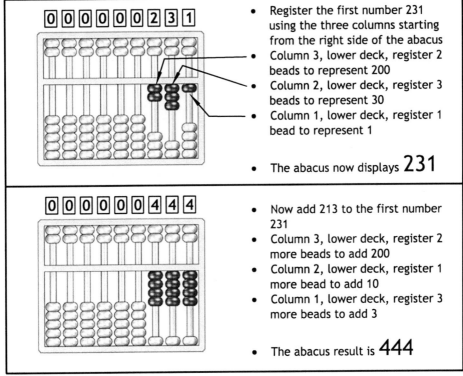

- Register the first number 231 using the three columns starting from the right side of the abacus
- Column 3, lower deck, register 2 beads to represent 200
- Column 2, lower deck, register 3 beads to represent 30
- Column 1, lower deck, register 1 bead to represent 1

- The abacus now displays 231

- Now add 213 to the first number 231
- Column 3, lower deck, register 2 more beads to add 200
- Column 2, lower deck, register 1 more bead to add 10
- Column 1, lower deck, register 3 more beads to add 3

- The abacus result is 444

Figure 3.1

Adding two numbers that have different amounts of digits i.e. 2112 + 32.

- It is best to start with the number that has the largest amount of digits, in this case 2112.
- Then add the number with the smaller amount of digits, in this case 32, to the first number.

Example: 2112 + 32

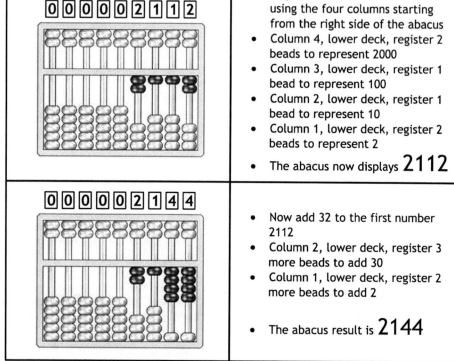

000002112	• Register the first number 2112 using the four columns starting from the right side of the abacus • Column 4, lower deck, register 2 beads to represent 2000 • Column 3, lower deck, register 1 bead to represent 100 • Column 2, lower deck, register 1 bead to represent 10 • Column 1, lower deck, register 2 beads to represent 2 • The abacus now displays **2112**
000002144	• Now add 32 to the first number 2112 • Column 2, lower deck, register 3 more beads to add 30 • Column 1, lower deck, register 2 more beads to add 2 • The abacus result is **2144**

Figure 3.2

Example: 6421 + 425

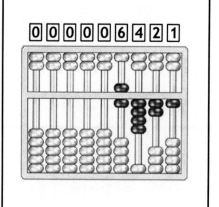

000006421	• Register the first number 6421 using the four columns starting from the right side of the abacus
	• Column 4:
	    upper deck, register 1 bead to represent 5000
	    lower deck, register 1 bead to represent 1000
	    (Total in column 4 is 5000 + 1000 = 6000)
	• Column 3, lower deck, register 4 beads to represent 400
	• Column 2, lower deck, register 2 beads to represent 20
	• Column 1, lower deck, register 1 bead to represent 1
	
	• The abacus now displays **6421**

Figure 3.3

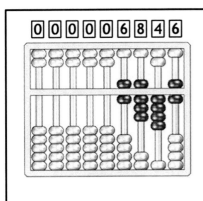

The addition of 425 to the first number 6421 is done in the following way:

- Column 3:
  upper deck, register 1 bead to add 500
  lower deck, unregister 1 bead to minus 100
  (Total in column 3 is 500 - 100 = 400)
- Column 2, lower deck, register 2 beads to add 20
- Column 1, upper deck, register 1 bead to add 5
- The abacus result is **6846**

Figure 3.3 (continued)

When there are not enough beads left in a column to make the addition, use a bead in the next left column to help.

When there are not enough beads in the column for the addition

Example: 8 + 4

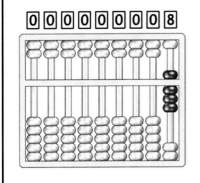

- Register the first number 8 using the first column starting from the right side of the abacus
- Column 1:
  upper deck, register 1 bead to represent 5
  lower deck, register 3 beads to represent 3
  (Total in column 1 is 5 + 3 = 8)
- The abacus now displays **8**

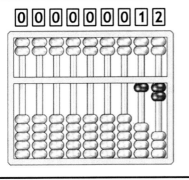

Now add 4 in the following way:
- There are not enough beads in column 1 to add 4, think 4 = 10 - 6, so remove 6 from column 1 and then add 10 in column 2
  Column 1:
  upper deck, unregister 1 bead to subtract 5
  lower deck, unregister 1 bead to subtract 1

  Column 2, lower deck, register 1 bead to add 10
  (Total is 10 - 5 - 1 = 4)
- The abacus result is **12**

Figure 3.4

Example: 9 + 5

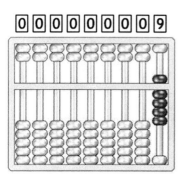

	• Register the first number 9 using the first column starting from the right side of the abacus • Column 1: upper deck, register 1 bead to represent 5 lower deck, register 4 beads to represent 4 (Total in column 1 is 5 + 4 = 9) • The abacus now displays **9**

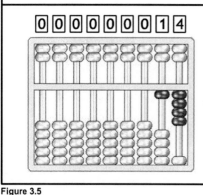

	Now add 5 in the following way: • There are not enough beads in column 1 to add 5, think 5 = 10 - 5, so remove 5 from column 1 and then add 10 in column 2 Column 1, upper deck, unregister 1 bead to subtract 5 Column 2, lower deck, register 1 bead to add 10 (Total is 10 - 5 = 5) • The abacus result is **14**

Figure 3.5

Example: 156 + 263

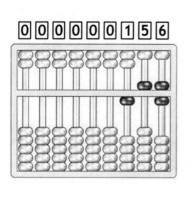

	• Register the first number 156 using the three columns starting from the right side of the abacus • Column 3, lower deck, register 1 bead to represent 100 • Column 2, upper deck, register 1 bead to represent 50 • Column 1: upper deck, register 1 bead to represent 5 lower deck, register 1 bead to represent 1 (Total in column 1 is 5 + 1 = 6) • The abacus now displays **156**

Figure 3.6

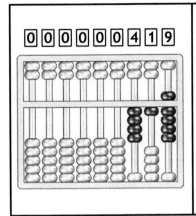

	The addition of 263 is done in the following way:
	• Column 3, lower deck, register 2 beads to add 200
	• There are not enough beads in column 2 to register 6 (to add 60), think 6 = 10 - 4
	Column 2, upper deck, unregister 1 bead to subtract 50, lower deck, register 1 bead to add 10
	Column 3, lower deck, register 1 bead to add 100 (Total is 100 - 50 + 10 = 60)
	• Column 1, lower deck, register 3 beads to add 3
	• The abacus result is **419**

Figure 3.6 (continued)

Skipped columns

When a column does not have enough beads left to make the addition in either the upper or lower deck, use the next left column to complete the addition. Sometimes this **next** column does not have any beads left to use, therefore the column must be **skipped** and you must move again to the next left column until you reach a column that has usable beads (beads that are not yet registered). Remember to unregister all the beads in the columns that you **skipped** over before you move to the next left column.

Example: 995 + 9

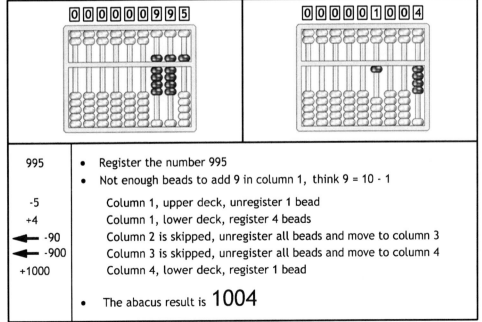

995	• Register the number 995
	• Not enough beads to add 9 in column 1, think 9 = 10 - 1
-5	Column 1, upper deck, unregister 1 bead
+4	Column 1, lower deck, register 4 beads
⬅ -90	Column 2 is skipped, unregister all beads and move to column 3
⬅ -900	Column 3 is skipped, unregister all beads and move to column 4
+1000	Column 4, lower deck, register 1 bead
	• The abacus result is **1004**

Figure 3.7

Various addition examples

Example: 4 + 5

4	• Register the number 4
+5	• Column 1, upper deck, register 1 bead
	• The abacus result is **9**

Figure 3.8

Example: 56 + 23

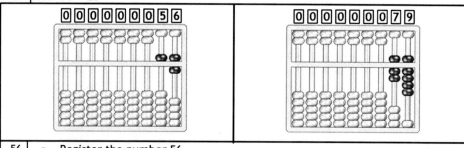

56	• Register the number 56
+20	• Column 2, lower deck, register 2 beads
+3	• Column 1, lower deck, register 3 beads
	• The abacus result is **79**

Figure 3.9

Example: 527 + 462

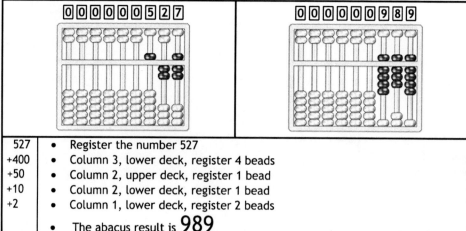

527	• Register the number 527
+400	• Column 3, lower deck, register 4 beads
+50	• Column 2, upper deck, register 1 bead
+10	• Column 2, lower deck, register 1 bead
+2	• Column 1, lower deck, register 2 beads
	• The abacus result is **989**

Figure 3.10

Example: 45 + 5

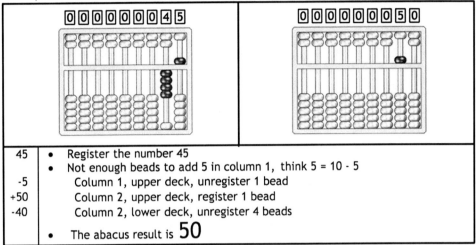

45	• Register the number 45
	• Not enough beads to add 5 in column 1, think 5 = 10 - 5
-5	Column 1, upper deck, unregister 1 bead
+50	Column 2, upper deck, register 1 bead
-40	Column 2, lower deck, unregister 4 beads
	• The abacus result is **50**

Figure 3.11

Example: 204 + 173

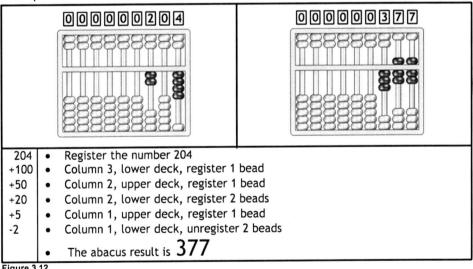

204	• Register the number 204
+100	• Column 3, lower deck, register 1 bead
+50	• Column 2, upper deck, register 1 bead
+20	• Column 2, lower deck, register 2 beads
+5	• Column 1, upper deck, register 1 bead
-2	• Column 1, lower deck, unregister 2 beads
	• The abacus result is **377**

Figure 3.12

Example: 65260 + 4539

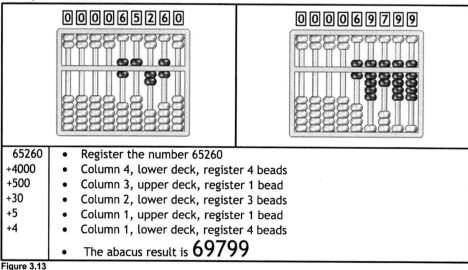

65260	• Register the number 65260
+4000	• Column 4, lower deck, register 4 beads
+500	• Column 3, upper deck, register 1 bead
+30	• Column 2, lower deck, register 3 beads
+5	• Column 1, upper deck, register 1 bead
+4	• Column 1, lower deck, register 4 beads
	• The abacus result is **69799**

Figure 3.13

Example: 523602092 + 425160905

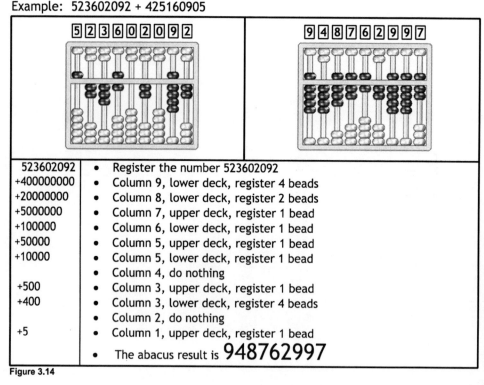

523602092	• Register the number 523602092
+400000000	• Column 9, lower deck, register 4 beads
+20000000	• Column 8, lower deck, register 2 beads
+5000000	• Column 7, upper deck, register 1 bead
+100000	• Column 6, lower deck, register 1 bead
+50000	• Column 5, upper deck, register 1 bead
+10000	• Column 5, lower deck, register 1 bead
	• Column 4, do nothing
+500	• Column 3, upper deck, register 1 bead
+400	• Column 3, lower deck, register 4 beads
	• Column 2, do nothing
+5	• Column 1, upper deck, register 1 bead
	• The abacus result is **948762997**

Figure 3.14

Example: 5395607 + 2803721

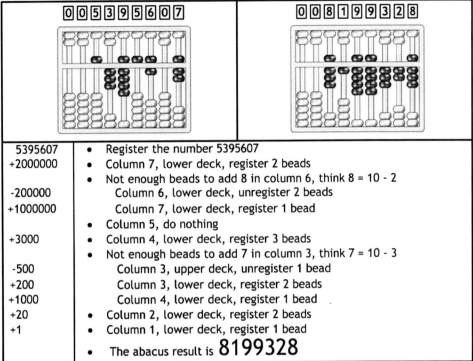

5395607	• Register the number 5395607
+2000000	• Column 7, lower deck, register 2 beads
	• Not enough beads to add 8 in column 6, think 8 = 10 - 2
-200000	Column 6, lower deck, unregister 2 beads
+1000000	Column 7, lower deck, register 1 bead
	• Column 5, do nothing
+3000	• Column 4, lower deck, register 3 beads
	• Not enough beads to add 7 in column 3, think 7 = 10 - 3
-500	Column 3, upper deck, unregister 1 bead
+200	Column 3, lower deck, register 2 beads
+1000	Column 4, lower deck, register 1 bead
+20	• Column 2, lower deck, register 2 beads
+1	• Column 1, lower deck, register 1 bead
	• The abacus result is **8199328**

Figure 3.15

Example: 123456789 + 121521210

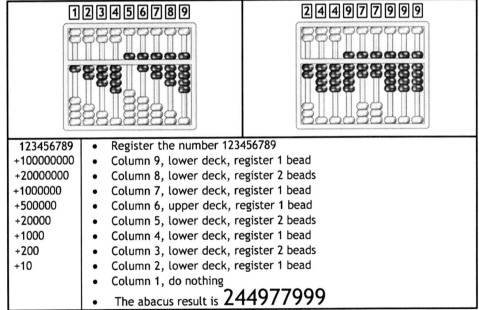

123456789	• Register the number 123456789
+100000000	• Column 9, lower deck, register 1 bead
+20000000	• Column 8, lower deck, register 2 beads
+1000000	• Column 7, lower deck, register 1 bead
+500000	• Column 6, upper deck, register 1 bead
+20000	• Column 5, lower deck, register 2 beads
+1000	• Column 4, lower deck, register 1 bead
+200	• Column 3, lower deck, register 2 beads
+10	• Column 2, lower deck, register 1 bead
	• Column 1, do nothing
	• The abacus result is **244977999**

Figure 3.16

Example: 99999 + 11111

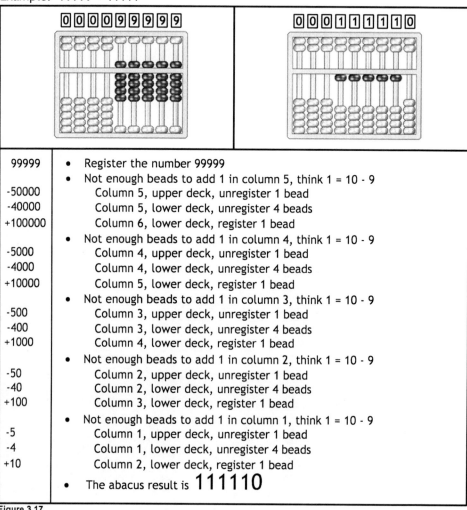

99999	• Register the number 99999
	• Not enough beads to add 1 in column 5, think 1 = 10 - 9
-50000	Column 5, upper deck, unregister 1 bead
-40000	Column 5, lower deck, unregister 4 beads
+100000	Column 6, lower deck, register 1 bead
	• Not enough beads to add 1 in column 4, think 1 = 10 - 9
-5000	Column 4, upper deck, unregister 1 bead
-4000	Column 4, lower deck, unregister 4 beads
+10000	Column 5, lower deck, register 1 bead
	• Not enough beads to add 1 in column 3, think 1 = 10 - 9
-500	Column 3, upper deck, unregister 1 bead
-400	Column 3, lower deck, unregister 4 beads
+1000	Column 4, lower deck, register 1 bead
	• Not enough beads to add 1 in column 2, think 1 = 10 - 9
-50	Column 2, upper deck, unregister 1 bead
-40	Column 2, lower deck, unregister 4 beads
+100	Column 3, lower deck, register 1 bead
	• Not enough beads to add 1 in column 1, think 1 = 10 - 9
-5	Column 1, upper deck, unregister 1 bead
-4	Column 1, lower deck, unregister 4 beads
+10	Column 2, lower deck, register 1 bead
	• The abacus result is **111110**

Figure 3.17

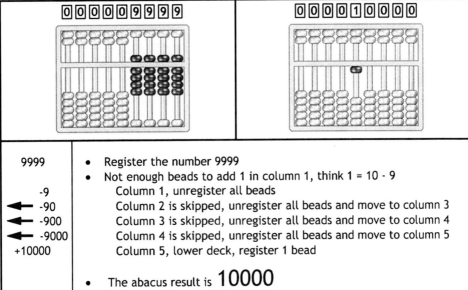

Example: 9999 + 1

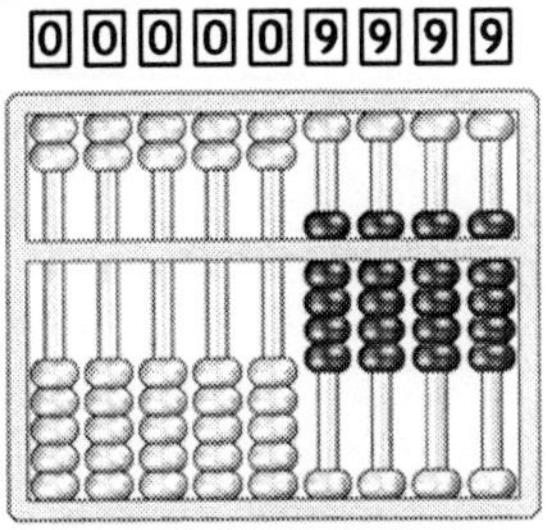

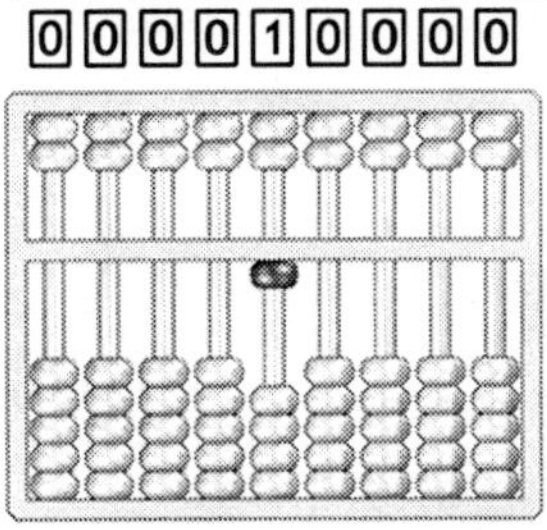

9999	• Register the number 9999
	• Not enough beads to add 1 in column 1, think 1 = 10 - 9
-9	Column 1, unregister all beads
← -90	Column 2 is skipped, unregister all beads and move to column 3
← -900	Column 3 is skipped, unregister all beads and move to column 4
← -9000	Column 4 is skipped, unregister all beads and move to column 5
+10000	Column 5, lower deck, register 1 bead
	• The abacus result is **10000**

Figure 3.18

Addition of more than two numbers

When making additions of multiple numbers, just find the sum of the first two numbers, then add on the next number to get the new sum, the following number can then be added to this to get the next sum etc..
Continue to add one number to the sum of the previous numbers until all the numbers have been added.

Example: 123 + 254 + 522
First add 123 to 254 to get the sum, then add 522 to this sum to get the final sum.

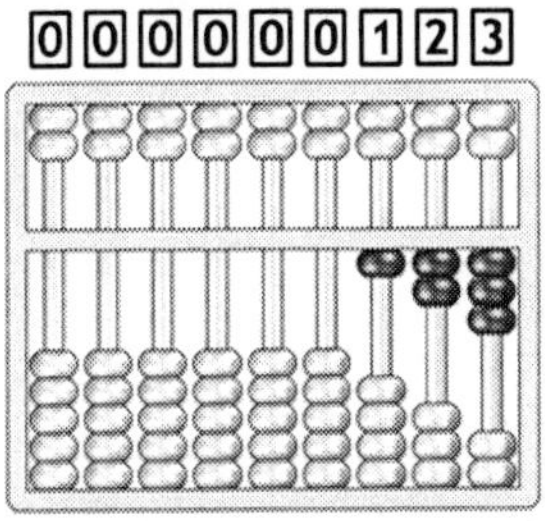

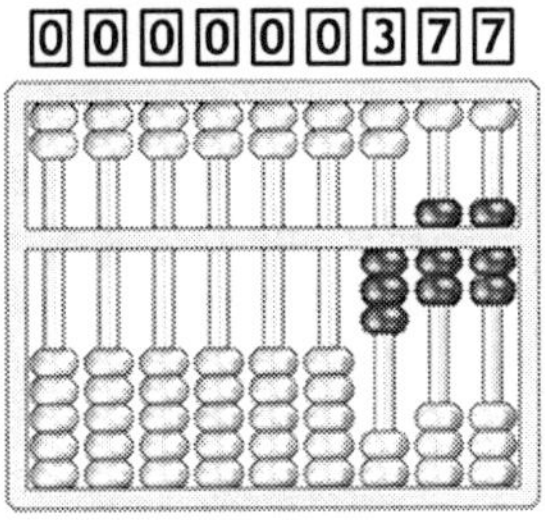

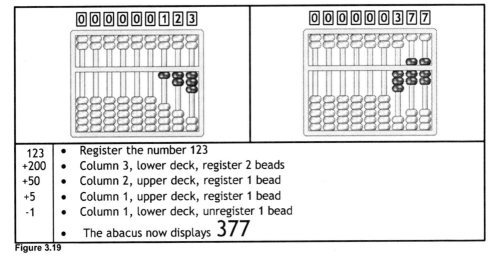

123	• Register the number 123
+200	• Column 3, lower deck, register 2 beads
+50	• Column 2, upper deck, register 1 bead
+5	• Column 1, upper deck, register 1 bead
-1	• Column 1, lower deck, unregister 1 bead
	• The abacus now displays **377**

Figure 3.19

Example: 123 + 254 + 522 (continued)

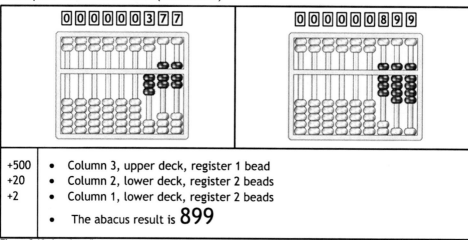

+500	• Column 3, upper deck, register 1 bead
+20	• Column 2, lower deck, register 2 beads
+2	• Column 1, lower deck, register 2 beads
	• The abacus result is **899**

Figure 3.19 (continued)

Example: 525631 + 253160 + 1210
First add 525631 to 253160 to get the sum

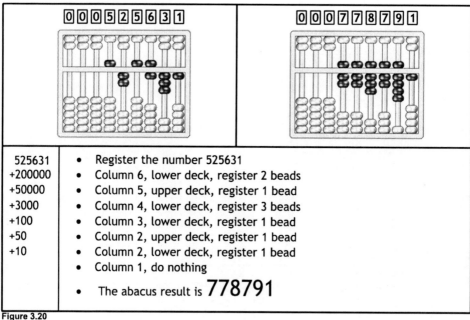

525631	• Register the number 525631
+200000	• Column 6, lower deck, register 2 beads
+50000	• Column 5, upper deck, register 1 bead
+3000	• Column 4, lower deck, register 3 beads
+100	• Column 3, lower deck, register 1 bead
+50	• Column 2, upper deck, register 1 bead
+10	• Column 2, lower deck, register 1 bead
	• Column 1, do nothing
	• The abacus result is **778791**

Figure 3.20

Example: 525631 + 253160 + 1210 (continued)

Now add 1210 to 778791 to get the final sum

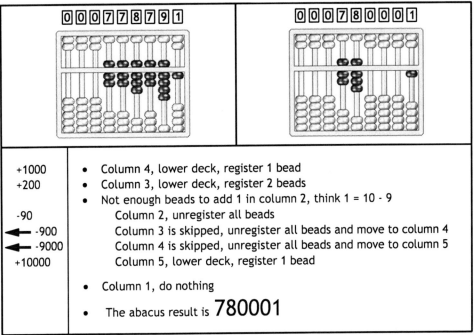

+1000
+200
 	
-90
← -900
← -9000
+10000
	• Column 4, lower deck, register 1 bead
	• Column 3, lower deck, register 2 beads
	• Not enough beads to add 1 in column 2, think 1 = 10 - 9
	    Column 2, unregister all beads
	    Column 3 is skipped, unregister all beads and move to column 4
	    Column 4 is skipped, unregister all beads and move to column 5
	    Column 5, lower deck, register 1 bead
	
	• Column 1, do nothing
	
	• The abacus result is **780001**

Figure 3.21

Addition with numbers that contain decimals.

A whole number is called an integer. A part of a whole number is called a non-integer or more commonly known as a decimal.

For example:

Take the number 36.48, the digits 3 and 6 are integers and the digits (on the right of the decimal point) 4 and 8 are decimals. Some abaci do not have a way to identify the decimal point therefore when adding numbers that contain decimals there are two methods to solve the problem.

Method 1: Use the decimal point marker on your abacus or if it doesn't have a marker you must remember the position of the decimal point.

Method 2: Move the decimal point in your numbers to change the decimal numbers to whole numbers.

Examples using method 1:
32.13 + 12.2

When adding the numbers it is important to remember to keep the digits in the correct columns. It is best to start with the number that has the most decimals.

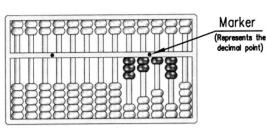

Marker
(Represents the decimal point)

Figure 3.22

28

Example: 32.13 + 12.2

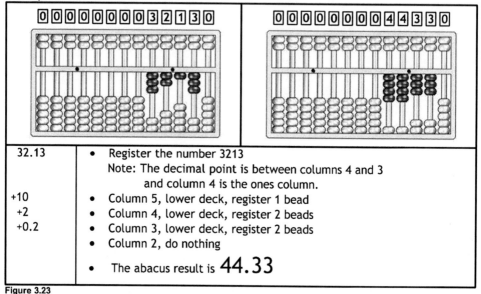

32.13	• Register the number 3213 Note: The decimal point is between columns 4 and 3 and column 4 is the ones column.
+10	• Column 5, lower deck, register 1 bead
+2	• Column 4, lower deck, register 2 beads
+0.2	• Column 3, lower deck, register 2 beads
	• Column 2, do nothing
	• The abacus result is **44.33**

Figure 3.23

Example: 64.374 + 9.32

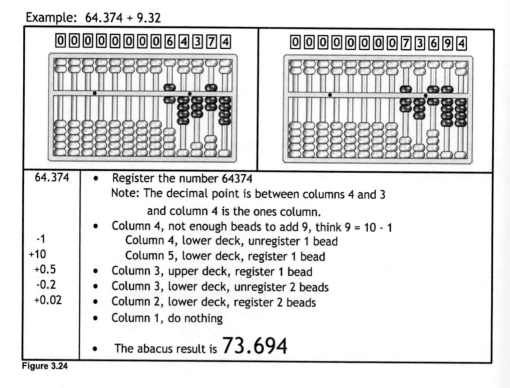

64.374	• Register the number 64374 Note: The decimal point is between columns 4 and 3 and column 4 is the ones column.
	• Column 4, not enough beads to add 9, think 9 = 10 - 1
-1	Column 4, lower deck, unregister 1 bead
+10	Column 5, lower deck, register 1 bead
+0.5	• Column 3, upper deck, register 1 bead
-0.2	• Column 3, lower deck, unregister 2 beads
+0.02	• Column 2, lower deck, register 2 beads
	• Column 1, do nothing
	• The abacus result is **73.694**

Figure 3.24

Example using method 2:
236.42 + 21.6

With this method we will be moving the decimal point.
The number that contains the most decimals is 236.42 and to make this number a
whole number the decimal point must be moved two places to the right to make
23642. Therefore the number that is going to be added to it must also have its
decimal point moved two places to the right to make 2160.
The calculation on the abacus now becomes 23642 + 2160. The result of this addition
reads 25802 on the abacus and now the decimal point must be put back into this
answer. Because the decimal point was moved two places to the right on both
numbers the answer must have the decimal point put back in at two places from the
left, so 25802 becomes 258.02 as the real answer.

Examples

Question	Move the decimal point	To be put into the abacus	Abacus answer	Put the decimal point back into the answer	Real answer
21.6 + 0.21	21.60 + 0.21 2 places 2 places	2160 + 21	2181	2181.0 2 places	21.81
0.04 + 0.0002	0.0400 + 0.0002 4 places 4 places	400 + 2	402	402.0 4 places	0.0402
6.21 + 800.043	6.210 + 800.043 3 places 3 places	6210 + 800043	806253	806253.0 3 places	806.253

Table 3.1

Questions | **Find the sum of the following:**
(see page 136 & 137 for the answers)

Question	Find the sum
1	58 + 45
2	564 + 135
3	885 + 9
4	5253 + 3231
5	55227 + 11111
6	732689 + 555201
7	4321543 + 5365
8	1535 + 252 + 22
9	135254 + 2560 + 125 + 52151
10	12345678 + 10000009 + 91255450
11	62.371 + 2.14
12	402.617 + 81.7

PART 4

SUBTRACTION

Subtraction 4

Subtraction is subtracting one (or more numbers) from another to find the difference.

When performing subtraction on the abacus:
- The numbers are registered on the abacus from the left side to the right side.
- Each digit must be entered in the correct column.
  For example, when subtracting two numbers that have three digits each, start by registering the first number in the first three columns then make the subtraction of the second number, again in the first three columns.
- When making a subtraction with multiple numbers it is important to know if the answer will be positive or negative, as there is no sign on the abacus to indicate this.

Example: 432 - 221

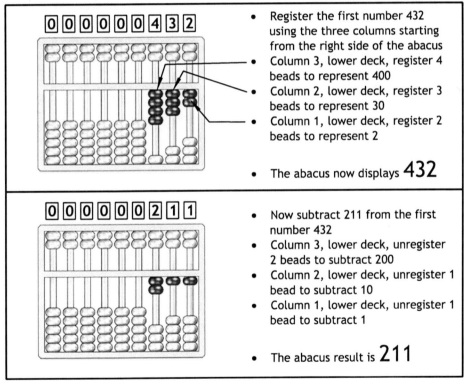

- Register the first number 432 using the three columns starting from the right side of the abacus
- Column 3, lower deck, register 4 beads to represent 400
- Column 2, lower deck, register 3 beads to represent 30
- Column 1, lower deck, register 2 beads to represent 2

- The abacus now displays 432

- Now subtract 211 from the first number 432
- Column 3, lower deck, unregister 2 beads to subtract 200
- Column 2, lower deck, unregister 1 bead to subtract 10
- Column 1, lower deck, unregister 1 bead to subtract 1

- The abacus result is 211

Figure 4.1

Subtracting two numbers that have different amounts of digits

Example: 4234 - 21

- It is best to start with the number that has the largest amount of digits, in this case 4234.
- Then subtract the number with the smaller amount of digits, in this case 21, from the first number.

Example: 4234 - 21

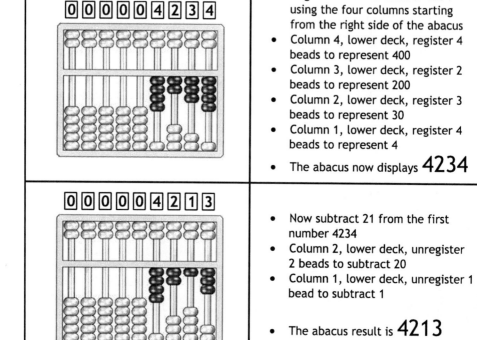

0 0 0 0 0 4 2 3 4	• Register the first number 4234 using the four columns starting from the right side of the abacus • Column 4, lower deck, register 4 beads to represent 400 • Column 3, lower deck, register 2 beads to represent 200 • Column 2, lower deck, register 3 beads to represent 30 • Column 1, lower deck, register 4 beads to represent 4 • The abacus now displays **4234**
0 0 0 0 0 4 2 1 3	• Now subtract 21 from the first number 4234 • Column 2, lower deck, unregister 2 beads to subtract 20 • Column 1, lower deck, unregister 1 bead to subtract 1 • The abacus result is **4213**

Figure 4.2

Example: 6533 - 323

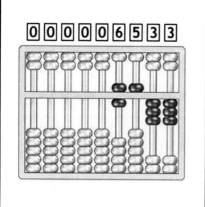

0 0 0 0 0 6 5 3 3	• Register the first number 6533 using the four columns starting from the right side of the abacus • Column 4: upper deck, register 1 bead to represent 5000 lower deck, register 1 bead to represent 1000 (Total in column 4 is 5000 + 1000 = 6000) • Column 3, upper deck, register 1 bead to represent 500 • Column 2, lower deck, register 3 beads to represent 30 • Column 1, lower deck, register 3 beads to represent 3 • The abacus now displays **6533**

Figure 4.3

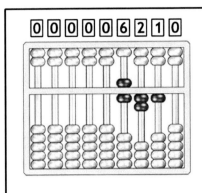

The subtraction of 323 from the first number 6533 is done in the following way:

- Column 3
  upper deck, unregister 1 bead to subtract 500
  lower deck, register 2 beads to add 200
  (Total in column 3 is -500 + 200 = -300)
- Column 2, lower deck, unregister 2 beads to subtract 20
- Column 1, lower deck, unregister 3 beads to subtract 3
- The abacus result is 6210

Figure 4.3 (continued)

When there are not enough beads left in a column to make the subtraction, use a bead in the next left column to help.

When there are not enough beads in the column for the subtraction

Example: 12 - 8

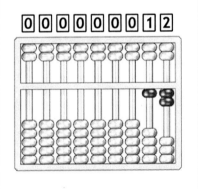

- Register the first number 12 using the first two columns starting from the right side of the abacus
- Column 2, lower deck, register 1 bead to represent 10
- Column 1, lower deck, register 2 beads to represent 2
- The abacus now displays 12

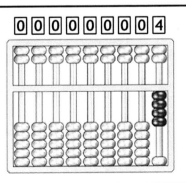

Now subtract 8 in the following way:
- Because there are not enough beads in column 1, move to the next left column to help.
  Column 2, lower deck, unregister 1 bead to subtract 10
- Column 1, lower deck, register 2 beads to add 2
  (Total is -10 + 2 = -8)
- The abacus result is 4

Figure 4.4

Example: 25 - 16

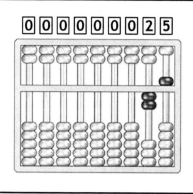

- Register the first number 25 using the first two columns starting from the right side of the abacus
- Column 2, lower deck, register 2 beads to represent 20
- Column 1, upper deck, register 1 bead to represent 5
- The abacus now displays **25**

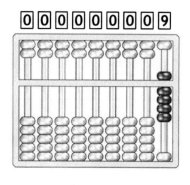

Now subtract 16 in the following way:
- Column 2, lower deck, unregister 1 bead to subtract 10
- Because there are not enough beads in the first column to subtract 6, move to the next left column to help.
- Column 2, lower deck, unregister 1 bead to subtract 10
- Column 1, lower deck, register 4 beads to add 4
- The abacus result is **9**

Figure 4.5

Example: 463 - 386

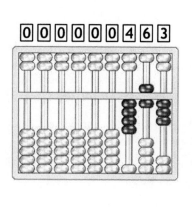

- Register the first number 463 using the first three columns starting from the right side of the abacus
- Column 3, lower deck, register 4 beads to represent 400
- Column 2:
    - upper deck, register 1 bead to represent 50
    - lower deck, register 1 bead to represent 10
    - (Total is 50 + 10 = 60)
- Column 1, lower deck, register 3 beads to represent 3
- The abacus now displays **463**

Figure 4.6

	The subtraction of 386 is done in the following way:

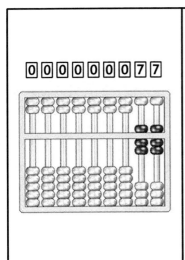	• Column 3, lower deck, unregister 3 beads to subtract 300
	• There are not enough beads in column 2 to subtract 8, therefore move to column 3:
	  Column 3, lower deck, unregister 1 bead to subtract 100, now move back to column 2
	  Column 2, lower deck, register 2 beads to add 20 (Total is -100 + 20 = -80)
	• There are not enough beads in column 1 to subtract 6, therefore move to column 2:
	• Column 2, lower deck, unregister 1 bead to subtract 10, now move back to column 1
	  Column 1, upper deck, register 1 bead to add 5
	  Column 1, lower deck, unregister 1 bead to subtract 1 (Total is -10 + 5 - 1 = -6)
	• The abacus result is 77

Figure 4.6 (continued)

Skipped columns

When a column does not have enough beads left to make the subtraction in either the upper or lower deck, move to the next left column to continue with the subtraction. Sometimes this **next** column does not have any beads to use, therefore the column must be **skipped** and you must move again to the next left column until you reach a column that has usable beads (beads that are registered). Remember to register all the beads in the columns that you **skipped** over (1 bead in the upper deck and 4 beads in the lower deck) before you move to the next left column.

Example: 100 - 5

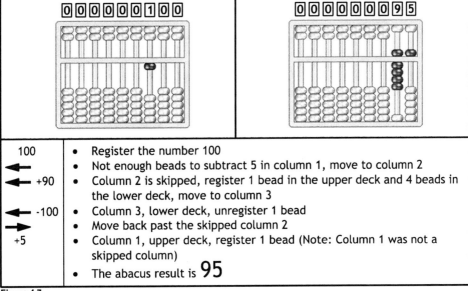

100 ← ← +90 ← -100 → +5	• Register the number 100 • Not enough beads to subtract 5 in column 1, move to column 2 • Column 2 is skipped, register 1 bead in the upper deck and 4 beads in the lower deck, move to column 3 • Column 3, lower deck, unregister 1 bead • Move back past the skipped column 2 • Column 1, upper deck, register 1 bead (Note: Column 1 was not a skipped column) • The abacus result is 95

Figure 4.7

Various subtraction examples

Example: 9 - 5

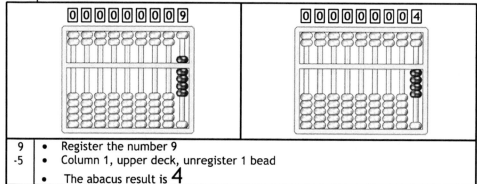

9	• Register the number 9
-5	• Column 1, upper deck, unregister 1 bead
	• The abacus result is **4**

Figure 4.8

Example: 87 - 21

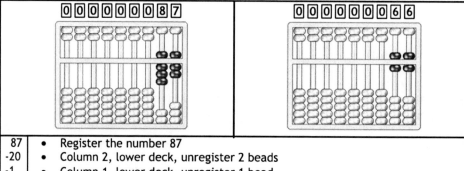

87	• Register the number 87
-20	• Column 2, lower deck, unregister 2 beads
-1	• Column 1, lower deck, unregister 1 bead
	• The abacus result is **66**

Figure 4.9

Example: 987 - 671

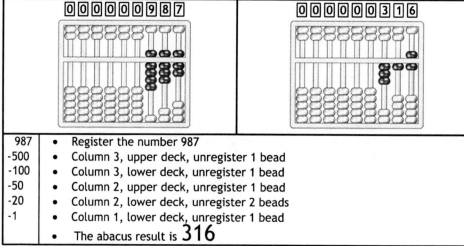

987	• Register the number 987
-500	• Column 3, upper deck, unregister 1 bead
-100	• Column 3, lower deck, unregister 1 bead
-50	• Column 2, upper deck, unregister 1 bead
-20	• Column 2, lower deck, unregister 2 beads
-1	• Column 1, lower deck, unregister 1 bead
	• The abacus result is **316**

Figure 4.10

Example: 10 - 5

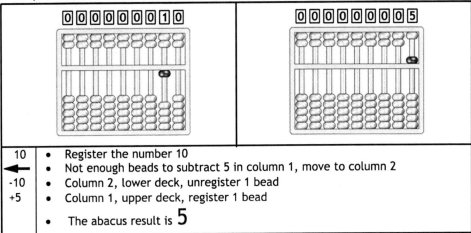

10	• Register the number 10
←	• Not enough beads to subtract 5 in column 1, move to column 2
-10	• Column 2, lower deck, unregister 1 bead
+5	• Column 1, upper deck, register 1 bead
	• The abacus result is 5

Figure 4.11

Example: 477 - 286

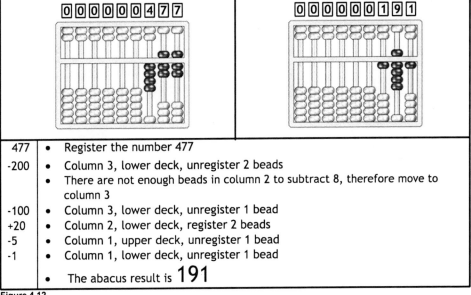

477	• Register the number 477
-200	• Column 3, lower deck, unregister 2 beads
	• There are not enough beads in column 2 to subtract 8, therefore move to column 3
-100	• Column 3, lower deck, unregister 1 bead
+20	• Column 2, lower deck, register 2 beads
-5	• Column 1, upper deck, unregister 1 bead
-1	• Column 1, lower deck, unregister 1 bead
	• The abacus result is 191

Figure 4.12

Example: 76205 - 5203

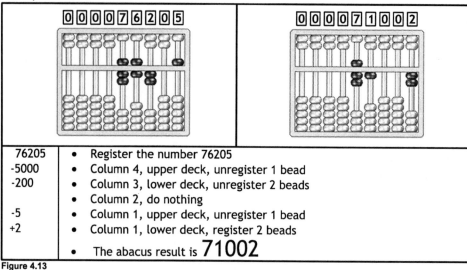

76205	• Register the number 76205
-5000	• Column 4, upper deck, unregister 1 bead
-200	• Column 3, lower deck, unregister 2 beads
	• Column 2, do nothing
-5	• Column 1, upper deck, unregister 1 bead
+2	• Column 1, lower deck, register 2 beads
	• The abacus result is **71002**

Figure 4.13

Example: 642603284 - 521502064

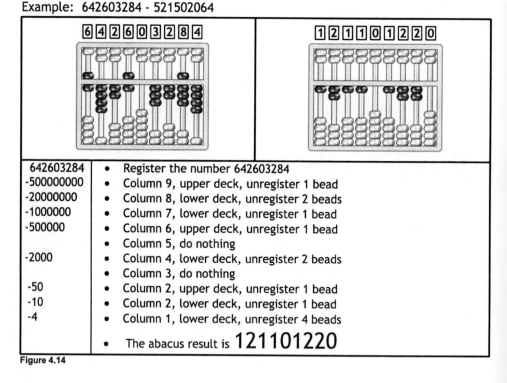

642603284	• Register the number 642603284
-500000000	• Column 9, upper deck, unregister 1 bead
-20000000	• Column 8, lower deck, unregister 2 beads
-1000000	• Column 7, lower deck, unregister 1 bead
-500000	• Column 6, upper deck, unregister 1 bead
	• Column 5, do nothing
-2000	• Column 4, lower deck, unregister 2 beads
	• Column 3, do nothing
-50	• Column 2, upper deck, unregister 1 bead
-10	• Column 2, lower deck, unregister 1 bead
-4	• Column 1, lower deck, unregister 4 beads
	• The abacus result is **121101220**

Figure 4.14

Example: 6495613 - 5530232

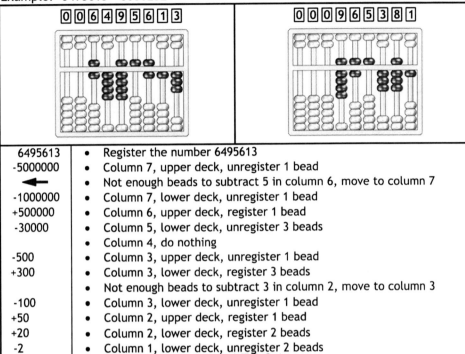

6495613	• Register the number 6495613
-5000000	• Column 7, upper deck, unregister 1 bead
←	• Not enough beads to subtract 5 in column 6, move to column 7
-1000000	• Column 7, lower deck, unregister 1 bead
+500000	• Column 6, upper deck, register 1 bead
-30000	• Column 5, lower deck, unregister 3 beads
	• Column 4, do nothing
-500	• Column 3, upper deck, unregister 1 bead
+300	• Column 3, lower deck, register 3 beads
	• Not enough beads to subtract 3 in column 2, move to column 3
-100	• Column 3, lower deck, unregister 1 bead
+50	• Column 2, upper deck, register 1 bead
+20	• Column 2, lower deck, register 2 beads
-2	• Column 1, lower deck, unregister 2 beads
	• The abacus result is **965381**

Figure 4.15

Example: 987654321 - 321550211

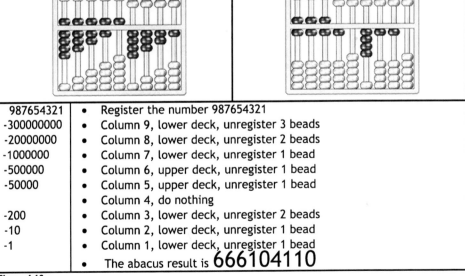

987654321	• Register the number 987654321
-300000000	• Column 9, lower deck, unregister 3 beads
-20000000	• Column 8, lower deck, unregister 2 beads
-1000000	• Column 7, lower deck, unregister 1 bead
-500000	• Column 6, upper deck, unregister 1 bead
-50000	• Column 5, upper deck, unregister 1 bead
	• Column 4, do nothing
-200	• Column 3, lower deck, unregister 2 beads
-10	• Column 2, lower deck, unregister 1 bead
-1	• Column 1, lower deck, unregister 1 bead
	• The abacus result is **666104110**

Figure 4.16

Example: 100000 - 11111

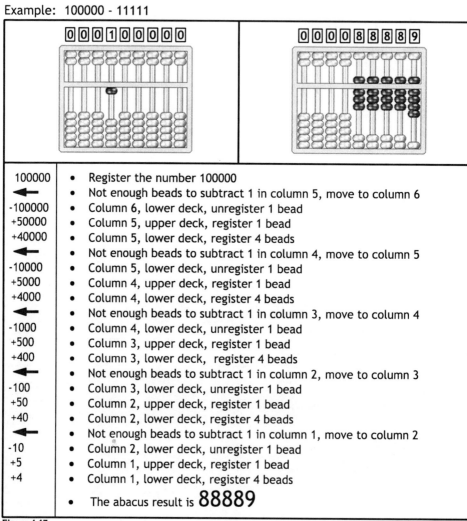

100000	• Register the number 100000
◄—	• Not enough beads to subtract 1 in column 5, move to column 6
-100000	• Column 6, lower deck, unregister 1 bead
+50000	• Column 5, upper deck, register 1 bead
+40000	• Column 5, lower deck, register 4 beads
◄—	• Not enough beads to subtract 1 in column 4, move to column 5
-10000	• Column 5, lower deck, unregister 1 bead
+5000	• Column 4, upper deck, register 1 bead
+4000	• Column 4, lower deck, register 4 beads
◄—	• Not enough beads to subtract 1 in column 3, move to column 4
-1000	• Column 4, lower deck, unregister 1 bead
+500	• Column 3, upper deck, register 1 bead
+400	• Column 3, lower deck, register 4 beads
◄—	• Not enough beads to subtract 1 in column 2, move to column 3
-100	• Column 3, lower deck, unregister 1 bead
+50	• Column 2, upper deck, register 1 bead
+40	• Column 2, lower deck, register 4 beads
◄—	• Not enough beads to subtract 1 in column 1, move to column 2
-10	• Column 2, lower deck, unregister 1 bead
+5	• Column 1, upper deck, register 1 bead
+4	• Column 1, lower deck, register 4 beads
	• The abacus result is **88889**

Figure 4.17

Example: 1000 - 1

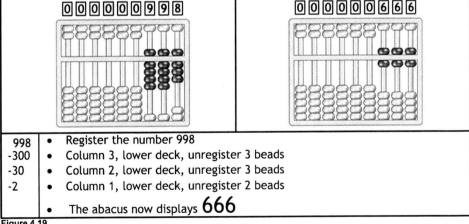

1000	• Register the number 1000
←	• Not enough beads to subtract 1 in column 1, move to column 2
← +90	• Column 2 is skipped, register 1 bead in the upper deck and 4 beads in the lower deck, move to column 3
← +900	• Column 3 is skipped, register 1 bead in the upper deck and 4 beads in the lower deck, move to column 4
-1000	• Column 4, lower deck unregister 1 bead
→	• Move back past the skipped column 3
→	• Move back past the skipped column 2
+5	• Column 1, upper deck, register 1 bead
+4	• Column 1, lower deck, register 4 beads
	• The abacus result is **999**

Figure 4.18

Subtraction of more than two numbers

When making subtractions of multiple numbers, just find the difference between the first two numbers, then subtract the next number to get the new difference, the following number can then be subtracted from this to get the next difference etc.. Continue to subtract one number from the difference of the previous numbers until all the numbers have been subtracted.

Example: 998 - 332 - 151

First subtract 332 from 998 to get the difference, then subtract 151 from this to get the final result.

998	• Register the number 998
-300	• Column 3, lower deck, unregister 3 beads
-30	• Column 2, lower deck, unregister 3 beads
-2	• Column 1, lower deck, unregister 2 beads
	• The abacus now displays **666**

Figure 4.19

Example: 998 - 332 - 151 (continued)

Now subtract 151 from 666 to get the final result

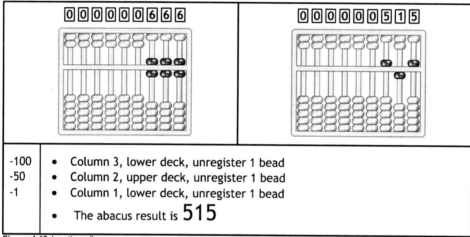

-100 -50 -1	• Column 3, lower deck, unregister 1 bead • Column 2, upper deck, unregister 1 bead • Column 1, lower deck, unregister 1 bead • The abacus result is **515**

Figure 4.19 (continued)

Example: 424662 - 212330 - 1240

First subtract 212330 from 424662 to get the difference

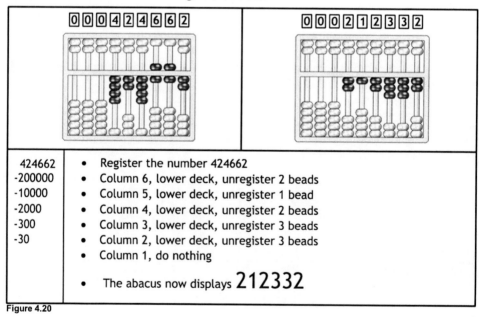

424662 -200000 -10000 -2000 -300 -30	• Register the number 424662 • Column 6, lower deck, unregister 2 beads • Column 5, lower deck, unregister 1 bead • Column 4, lower deck, unregister 2 beads • Column 3, lower deck, unregister 3 beads • Column 2, lower deck, unregister 3 beads • Column 1, do nothing • The abacus now displays **212332**

Figure 4.20

Example: 424662 - 212330 - 1240 (continued)
Now subtract 1240 from 212332 to get the final result.

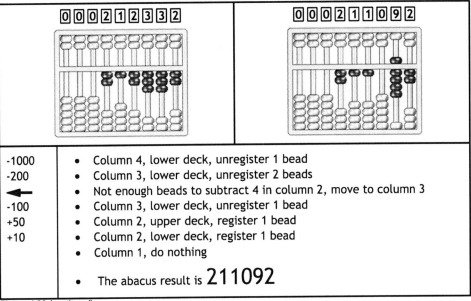

-1000	• Column 4, lower deck, unregister 1 bead
-200	• Column 3, lower deck, unregister 2 beads
←	• Not enough beads to subtract 4 in column 2, move to column 3
-100	• Column 3, lower deck, unregister 1 bead
+50	• Column 2, upper deck, register 1 bead
+10	• Column 2, lower deck, register 1 bead
	• Column 1, do nothing
	• The abacus result is **211092**

Figure 4.20 (continued)

Subtraction with numbers that contain decimals.

There are two methods of subtracting numbers that contain decimals.

Method 1: Use the decimal point marker on your abacus or if it doesn't have a marker you must remember the position of the decimal point.
Method 2: Move the decimal point in your numbers to change the decimal numbers into whole numbers.

Examples using method 1:
46.23 - 12.1

When subtracting the numbers it is important to remember to keep the digits in the correct columns. It is best to start with the number that has the most decimals.

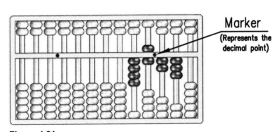

Marker
(Represents the decimal point)

Figure 4.21

Example: 46.23 - 12.1

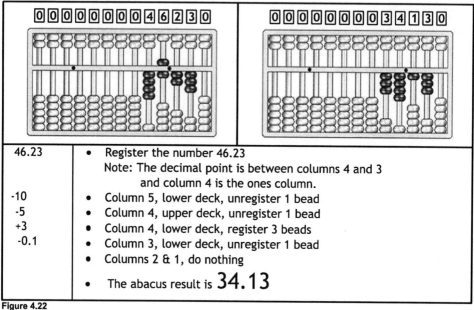

46.23	• Register the number 46.23
	Note: The decimal point is between columns 4 and 3
	and column 4 is the ones column.
-10	• Column 5, lower deck, unregister 1 bead
-5	• Column 4, upper deck, unregister 1 bead
+3	• Column 4, lower deck, register 3 beads
-0.1	• Column 3, lower deck, unregister 1 bead
	• Columns 2 & 1, do nothing
	• The abacus result is **34.13**

Figure 4.22

Example: 56.475 - 8.26

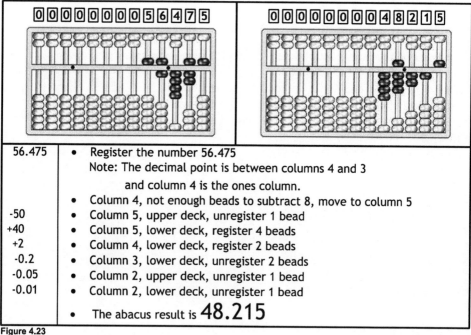

56.475	• Register the number 56.475
	Note: The decimal point is between columns 4 and 3
	and column 4 is the ones column.
	• Column 4, not enough beads to subtract 8, move to column 5
-50	• Column 5, upper deck, unregister 1 bead
+40	• Column 5, lower deck, register 4 beads
+2	• Column 4, lower deck, register 2 beads
-0.2	• Column 3, lower deck, unregister 2 beads
-0.05	• Column 2, upper deck, unregister 1 bead
-0.01	• Column 2, lower deck, unregister 1 bead
	• The abacus result is **48.215**

Figure 4.23

Example using method 2:
634.23 - 42.1

With this method we will be moving the decimal point.
The number that contains the most decimals is 634.23 and to make this number a whole number the decimal point must be moved two places to the right to make 63423. Therefore the number that is going to be subtracted from it must also have its decimal point moved two places to the right to make 4210.
The calculation on the abacus now becomes 63423 - 4210. The result of this subtraction reads 59213 on the abacus and now the decimal point must be put back into this answer. Because the decimal point was moved two places to the right on both numbers the answer must have the decimal point put back in at two places to the left, so 59213 becomes 592.13 as the real answer.

Examples

Question	Move the decimal point	To be put into the abacus	Abacus answer	Put the decimal point back into the answer	Real answer
45.6 - 0.19	45.60 - 0.19 2 places 2 places	4560 - 19	4541	4541.0 2 places	45.41
0.03 - 0.0002	0.0300 - 0.0002 4 places 4 places	300 - 2	298	298.0 4 places	0.0298
600.027 - 4.78	600.027 - 4.780 3 places 3 places	600027 - 4780	595247	595247.0 3 places	595.247

Table 4.1

Find the result of the subtraction for the following numbers:

(see page 138 & 139 for the answers)

Question	Find the result
1	92 - 35
2	645 - 232
3	814 - 8
4	4342 - 2312
5	66338 - 11223
6	635253 - 246062
7	5213634 - 6128
8	4536 - 224 - 12
9	440262 - 3201 - 435 - 6713
10	87654321 - 10000008 - 642107
11	65.2731 - 2.642
12	107.31646 - 92.64

PART 5

MULTIPLICATION

Multiplication 5

Multiplication is the process of multiplying one number by another.
The first number (the multiplicand), is multiplied by the second number (the multiplier), to obtain the result (the product).

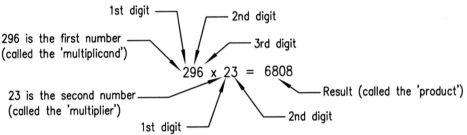

Figure 5.1

On the abacus, multiplication is slightly more complicated than performing addition and subtraction. The difficult part is to remember which column you are working on for each multiplication step, but with practice this will become easier.
There are many different ways in which to multiply on the abacus, some variations are:

1) Start by placing the multiplicand on the right side of the abacus and then place the multiplier on the left side.
2) Start by placing the multiplier on the right side of the abacus and then place the multiplicand on the left side.
3) Don't put either the multiplicand or multiplier on the abacus to start with.
4) Work by multiplying the digits from the left side to the right side.
5) Work by multiplying the digits from the right side to the left side.

In this chapter, the technique used will be to start by placing the multiplicand on the right side and the multiplier on the left side and work by multiplying the digits from the left side to the right side.

When multiplying on the abacus it is also essential to know by memory the multiplication tables at least from 1 x 1 up to 9 x 9 in order to help with your calculation (when dividing on the abacus it is essential to know from 1 x 1 to 12 x 12). Essentially the abacus is used to make the additions of each multiplication in order to get your result (product).

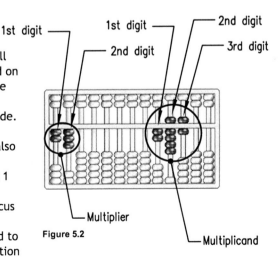

Figure 5.2

Multiplication tables from 1 x 1 to 12 x 12

	1	2	3	4	5	6	7	8	9	10	11	12
1	1	2	3	4	5	6	7	8	9	10	11	12
2	2	4	6	8	10	12	14	16	18	20	22	24
3	3	6	9	12	15	18	21	24	27	30	33	36
4	4	8	12	16	20	24	28	32	36	40	44	48
5	5	10	15	20	25	30	35	40	45	50	55	60
6	6	12	18	24	30	36	42	48	54	60	66	72
7	7	14	21	28	35	42	49	56	63	70	77	84
8	8	16	24	32	40	48	56	64	72	80	88	96
9	9	18	27	36	45	54	63	72	81	90	99	108
10	10	20	30	40	50	60	70	80	90	100	110	120
11	11	22	33	44	55	66	77	88	99	110	121	132
12	12	24	36	48	60	72	84	96	108	120	132	144

Table 5.1

How to use the multiplication table 5.1

Example, to find 6 x 8, use the column on the left-hand side to locate the first number 6 then move horizontally to the right until you find the number that is in column 8, in this case the number 48. This number (48) is the product of 6 x 8.

A note about the base column

When looking at the multiplication tables (see page 52) you can see that some of the results are single digit numbers i.e. 4 x 2 gives the result of a single digit number 8, whilst some are double digit numbers like the result of 8 x 6 which is 48.

The base column is the column that you start to enter the result. So if your base column is column 3 then entering a single digit result like 4 you would enter it in column 3 (see figure 5.3), but if your result was a double digit number like 42, you would start at the base column 3 but would use column 4 also i.e. the 4 would be registered in column 4 and the 2 in column 3 (see figure 5.4).

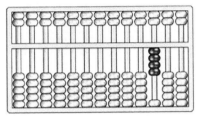

Figure 5.3

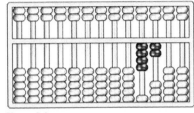

Figure 5.4

Note: Any beads that are already registered in the base column (or other columns) must be accounted for.

Example 1:
You are registering your new result of 6 into column 3, which already has 2 registered (see figure 5.5), just add your 6 (1 upper bead and 1 lower bead) to the existing 2, in this case giving a total of 8 in this column (see figure 5.6).

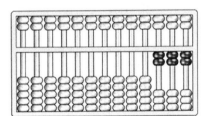

Figure 5.5

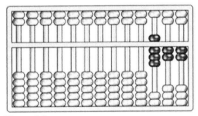

Figure 5.6

Example 2:

During your calculation (abacus reading 862 at this stage, see figure 5.7) you are registering your new result of 12 (actually 120 units) into base column 2, which already has 1 lower bead and 1 upper bead registered, this is the procedure:

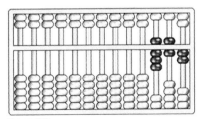

Figure 5.7

You know that your base column is column 2.

Add 12 by registering 1 lower bead in the next left column to the base column (same as adding 100 units to the abacus),

The abacus now reads 962 (which is 100 added onto 862), see figure 5.8.

Now register 2 lower beads in column 2, the base column (same as adding 20 units to the abacus).

The abacus now reads 982 (which is 20 added onto 962), see figure 5.9.

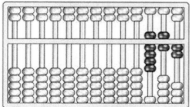

Figure 5.8

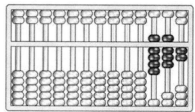

Figure 5.9

Which column should you use to enter your result?

The most complicated part of multiplying with the abacus is knowing which column you should be using to enter your result. When you are confused this is a quick way to remember.

Count the digits from the right side of the numbers that you are working on, for both the multiplicand and the multiplier and minus the result by 1.

This will tell you which column you should be working on (called the base column) to enter your result.

For example:

You are multiplying 6742 x 5831 and during your calculation of 6 x 8 (6 from the multiplicand and 8 from the multiplier) you have lost your position.

Just count the digits and minus 1.

i.e. 4 + 3 = 7 (fourth digit from the right of the multiplicand and the third digit from the right of the multiplier) now minus 1 to get 6. You should start with column 6 as your base column to enter your new result.

Quick test

Which column do you start with (the base column) to enter the result of multiplying the following digits?

(see page 140 for the answers)

Question	When calculating these numbers	When multiplying the following digits	Which column is your base column?
1	4321 x 3976	3 x 9	?
2	165 x 21	5 x 1	?
3	463 x 8	4 x 8	?
4	743215 x 68793	4 x 8	?
5	8176427 x 776431	6 x 6	?

Table 5.2

Digit sequence

In the following examples from this chapter the digits in all numbers, for both multiplicand and multiplier will be numbered in sequence from the left side as follows: Example, take the number 67412, the 6 will be called the first digit, the 7 will be the second digit and the 4 will be the third digit etc.

How to multiply on the abacus

Example: 21 x 34

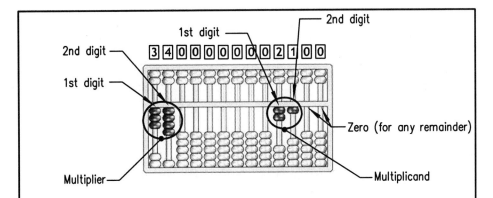

- Count the amount of digits in total (multiplier and multiplicand) in this case 4 digits (34 = 2 digits and 21 = 2 digits)
- Register the multiplicand (21) on the right side of the abacus (starting with the column which corresponds to the total amount of digits) i.e. 4 total digits, so start at column 4
- Place the multiplier (34) on the left side of the abacus

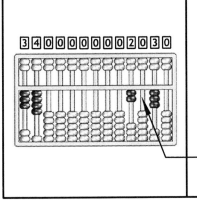

- Start with the second digit of the multiplicand (the right most digit) and multiply by the first digit of the multiplier (the left most digit)
- i.e. 21 x 34 first step is to multiply 1 x 3 (1 being the second digit of the multiplicand and 3 being the first digit of the multiplier) to get the result of 3
- Unregister the 2nd digit of the multiplicand (the 1 digit) before registering the result, this creates a gap between the multiplicand and the result.
- Enter the result (3) in column 2

Figure 5.10

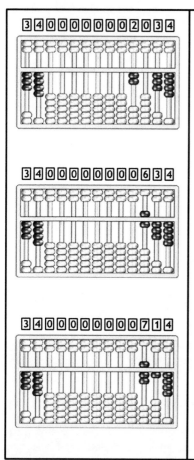

3 4 0 0 0 0 0 0 0 2 0 3 4	• Next, multiply the second digit of the multiplicand (1) with the second digit of the multiplier (4) to get 1 x 4 = 4
	• As we have moved one digit to the right of the multiplier we now move one column to the right on the abacus (column 1) to enter the next result of 4
	• Enter the result (4) in column 1
3 4 0 0 0 0 0 0 0 0 6 3 4	• Now multiply the first digit of the multiplicand (2) by the first digit of the multiplier (3) to get the next result, 2 x 3 = 6
	• Unregister the 1st digit of the multiplicand (the 2 digit) in column 4
	• Enter the result (6) in column 3
3 4 0 0 0 0 0 0 0 0 7 1 4	• Finally take the first digit of the multiplicand (2) multiply by the second digit of the multiplier (4) to get 2 x 4 = 8
	• As we have moved one digit to the right of the multiplier we now move one column to the right on the abacus (from column 3 to column 2) to enter the new result of 8
	• Enter the new result (8) in column 2 of the abacus, note that 3 is already registered in this column so add 8 to this to get 11, so unregister 2 beads, lower deck in column 2 then register 1 bead, lower deck in column 3
	• The final abacus result is **714**

Figure 5.10 (continued)

Examples of how to multiply with the abacus

Note: Throughout the examples the MulTiplier will be abbreviated to MT and the MultiplicanD to MD

Multiplying when the multiplier has one digit

Example: 43 x 2

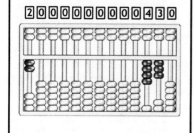

2 0 0 0 0 0 0 0 0 4 3 0	• Register the multiplier (MT) 2 on the left side of the abacus
	• Register the multiplicand (MD) 43 on the right side of the abacus, starting at the column equal to the total number of digits, in this case column 3

Figure 5.11

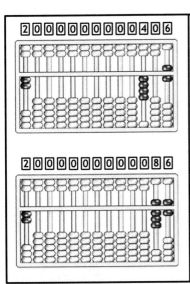

- 2nd digit of the MD is 3
- 1st digit of the MT is 2
- Base column is column 1
- 3 x 2 = 6, unregister the MD digit 3 in column 2
- Column 1 register 6

- 1st digit of the MD is 4
- 1st digit of the MT is 2
- Base column is column 2
- 4 x 2 = 8, unregister the MD digit 4 in column 3
- Column 2 register 8
- The abacus result is **86**

Figure 5.11 (continued)

Example: 102 x 3

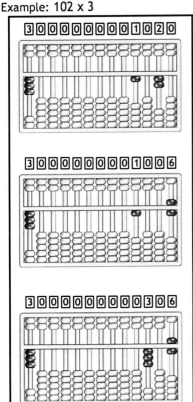

- Register the MT (3) on the left side of the abacus
- Register the MD (102) on the right side of the abacus, starting at the column equal to the total number of digits, in this case column 4

- 3rd digit of the MD is 2
- 1st digit of the MT is 3
- Base column is column 1
- 2 x 3 = 6, unregister the MD digit 2 in column 2
- column 1 register 6

- 2nd digit of the MD is 0
- 1st digit of the MT is 3
- Base column is column 2
- 0 x 3 = 0, column 2 do nothing

- 1st digit of the MD is 1
- 1st digit of the MT is 3
- Base column is column 3
- 1 x 3 = 3, unregister the MD digit 1 in column 4
- Column 3 register 3
- The abacus result is **306**

Figure 5.12

Example: 4635 x 8

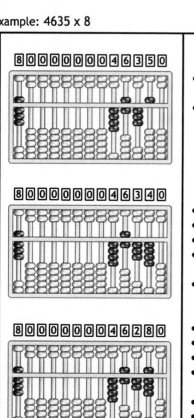

- Register the MT (8) on the left side of the abacus
- Register the MD (4635) on the right side of the abacus, starting at the column equal to the total number of digits, in this case column 5

- 4th digit of the MD is 5
- 1st digit of the MT is 8
- Base column is column 1
- 5 x 8 = 40, unregister the MD digit 5 in column 2
- Column 2 register 4, column 1 register 0

- 3rd digit of the MD is 3
- 1st digit of the MT is 8
- Base column is column 2
- 3 x 8 = 24, unregister the MD digit 3 in column 3
- Column 3 register 2
- Column 2 register 4 (add it to the already registered 4)

- 2nd digit of the MD is 6
- 1st digit of the MT is 8
- Base column is column 3
- 6 x 8 = 48, unregister the MD digit 6 in column 4
- Column 4 register 4
- Column 3 register 8 (add it to the already registered 2, use column 4 to help)

- 1st digit of the MD is 4
- 1st digit of the MT is 8
- Base column is column 4
- 4 x 8 = 32, unregister the MD digit 4 in column 5
- Column 5 register 3
- Column 4 register 2 (add it to the already registered 5)
- The abacus result is **37080**

Figure 5.13

Multiplying when the multiplier has two digits

Example: 23 x 14

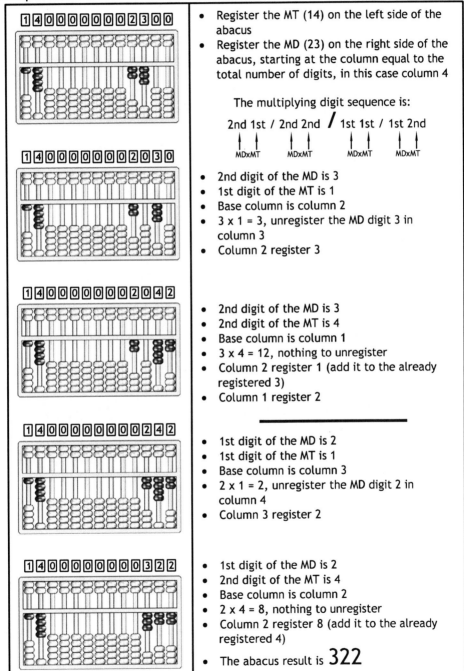

- Register the MT (14) on the left side of the abacus
- Register the MD (23) on the right side of the abacus, starting at the column equal to the total number of digits, in this case column 4

The multiplying digit sequence is:

2nd 1st / 2nd 2nd / 1st 1st / 1st 2nd

MDxMT   MDxMT   MDxMT   MDxMT

- 2nd digit of the MD is 3
- 1st digit of the MT is 1
- Base column is column 2
- 3 x 1 = 3, unregister the MD digit 3 in column 3
- Column 2 register 3

- 2nd digit of the MD is 3
- 2nd digit of the MT is 4
- Base column is column 1
- 3 x 4 = 12, nothing to unregister
- Column 2 register 1 (add it to the already registered 3)
- Column 1 register 2

- 1st digit of the MD is 2
- 1st digit of the MT is 1
- Base column is column 3
- 2 x 1 = 2, unregister the MD digit 2 in column 4
- Column 3 register 2

- 1st digit of the MD is 2
- 2nd digit of the MT is 4
- Base column is column 2
- 2 x 4 = 8, nothing to unregister
- Column 2 register 8 (add it to the already registered 4)
- The abacus result is **322**

Figure 5.14

Example: 296 x 23

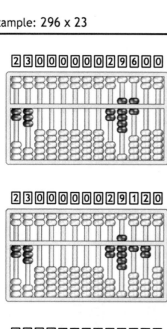

- Register the MT (23) on the left side of the abacus
- Register the MD (296) on the right side of the abacus, starting at the column equal to the total number of digits, in this case column 5

The multiplying digit sequence is:

3rd 1st / 3rd 2nd / 2nd 1st / 2nd 2nd / 1st 1st / 1st 2nd

- 3rd digit of the MD is 6
- 1st digit of the MT is 2
- Base column is column 2
- 6 x 2 = 12, unregister the MD digit 6 in column 3
- Column 3 register 1
- Column 2 register 2

- 3rd digit of the MD is 6
- 2nd digit of the MT is 3
- Base column is column 1
- 6 x 3 = 18, nothing to unregister
- Column 2 register 1 (add it to the already registered 2)
- Column 1 register 8

- 2nd digit of the MD is 9
- 1st digit of the MT is 2
- Base column is column 3
- 9 x 2 = 18, unregister the MD digit 9 in column 4
- Column 4 register 1
- Column 3 register 8 (add it to the already registered 1)

- 2nd digit of the MD is 9
- 2nd digit of the MT is 3
- Base column is column 2
- 9 x 3 = 27, nothing to unregister
- Column 3 register 2 (add it to the already registered 9)
- Column 2 register 7 (add it to the already registered 3)

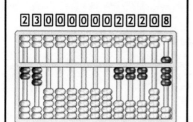

Figure 5.15

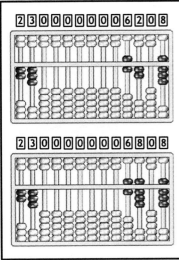

- 1st digit of the MD is 2
- 1st digit of the MT is 2
- Base column is column 4
- 2 x 2 = 4, unregister the MD digit 2 in column 5
- Column 4 register 4 (add it to the already registered 2)

- 1st digit of the MD is 2
- 2nd digit of the MT is 3
- Base column is column 3
- 2 x 3 = 6, nothing to unregister
- Column 3 register 6 (add it to the already registered 2)
- The abacus result is **6808**

Figure 5.15 (continued)

Multiplying with a multiplier that has three digits
Example: 234 x 185

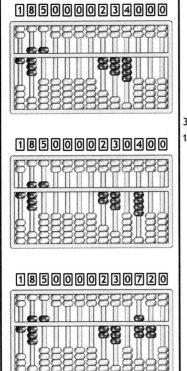

- Register the MT (185) on the left side of the abacus
- Register the MD (234) on the right side of the abacus, starting at the column equal to the total number of digits, in this case column 6

The multiplying digit sequence is:

3rd 1st / 3rd 2nd / 3rd 3rd / 2nd 1st / 2nd 2nd / 2nd 3rd /
1st 1st / 1st 2nd / 1st 3rd

- 3rd digit of the MD is 4
- 1st digit of the MT is 1
- Base column is column 3
- 4 x 1 = 4, unregister the MD digit 4 in column 4
- Column 3 register 4

- 3rd digit of the MD is 4
- 2nd digit of the MT is 8
- Base column is column 2
- 4 x 8 = 32, nothing to unregister
- Column 3 register 3 (add it to the already registered 4)
- Column 2 register 2

Figure 5.16

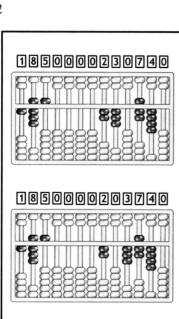

`1 8 5 0 0 0 0 2 3 0 7 4 0`

- 3rd digit of the MD is 4
- 3rd digit of the MT is 5
- Base column is column 1
- 4 x 5 = 20, nothing to unregister
- Column 2 register 2 (add it to the already registered 2)
- Column 1 do nothing

`1 8 5 0 0 0 0 2 0 3 7 4 0`

- 2nd digit of the MD is 3
- 1st digit of the MT is 1
- Base column is column 4
- 3 x 1 = 3, unregister the MD digit 3 in column 5
- Column 4 register 3

`1 8 5 0 0 0 0 2 0 6 1 4 0`

- 2nd digit of the MD is 3
- 2nd digit of the MT is 8
- Base column is column 3
- 3 x 8 = 24, nothing to unregister
- Column 4 register 2 (add it to the already registered 3)
- Column 3 register 4 (add it to the already registered 7)

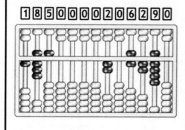

`1 8 5 0 0 0 0 2 0 6 2 9 0`

- 2nd digit of the MD is 3
- 3rd digit of the MT is 5
- Base column is column 2
- 3 x 5 = 15, nothing to unregister
- Column 3 register 1 (add it to the already registered 1)
- Column 2 register 5 (add it to the already registered 4)

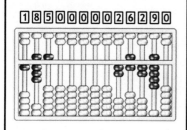

`1 8 5 0 0 0 0 0 2 6 2 9 0`

- 1st digit of the MD is 2
- 1st digit of the MT is 1
- Base column is column 5
- 2 x 1 = 2, unregister the MD digit 2 in column 6
- Column 5 register 2

Figure 5.16 (continued)

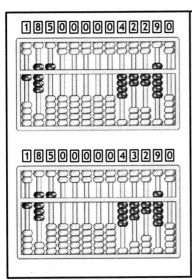

- 1st digit of the MD is 2
- 2nd digit of the MT is 8
- Base column is column 4
- 2 x 8 = 16, nothing to unregister
- Column 5 register 1 (add it to the already registered 2)
- Column 4 register 6 (add it to the already registered 6)

- 1st digit of the MD is 2
- 3rd digit of the MT is 5
- Base column is column 3
- 2 x 5 = 10, nothing to unregister
- Column 4 register 1 (add it to the already registered 2)
- Column 3 do nothing
- The abacus result is **43290**

Figure 5.16 (continued)

The same method that has been applied to the previous six examples can be applied to numbers with any amount of digits.

Multiplying when one of either the multiplier or multiplicand contains a decimal point

When multiplying and one of the numbers contains a decimal point do the following: Multiply both numbers as if they were integers, when you have found the product of the numbers, insert the decimal point in its correct position (count from the right side of the abacus).

Example:

281 x 12.63 = 3549.03
(Multiply on the abacus as 281 x 1263).
The decimal 12.63 has **two** decimal significant figures, so when the abacus result is 354903 (see figure 5.17) the decimal point is added **two** digits from the right side of the abacus to give the answer as 3549.03

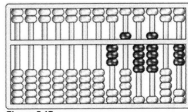

Figure 5.17

Further examples:

1) 62 x 3.4714 = 215.2268 (Multiply on the abacus as 62 x 34714).
   3.4714 has **four** significant figures so the abacus result 2152268 has to have the decimal point inserted **four** places from the right side of the abacus giving 215.2268 as the correct answer.

2) 4 x 21.721 = 86.884 (Multiply on the abacus as 4 x 21721).
   21.721 has **three** significant figures so the abacus result 86884 has to have the decimal point inserted **three** places from the right side of the abacus giving 86.884 as the correct answer.

Multiplying when both the multiplier and multiplicand contain a decimal point:

When multiplying two numbers that are both decimals, enter both numbers into the abacus as if they were integers.
Then when you have calculated the product you then insert your decimal point to get the correct answer.
The place to insert the decimal point is found by adding the total amount of decimal significant figures in both the multiplier and the multiplicand, then inserting the decimal point this amount of places from the right side of the abacus result.

Example:
64.36 x 2.6742 = 172.111512
(Multiply on the abacus as 6436 x 26742).

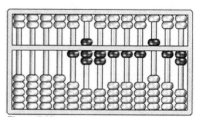

The decimal 64.36 has **two** decimal significant figures, and the decimal 2.6742 has **four** decimal significant figures so when the abacus result is 172111512 (see figure 5.18) the decimal point is placed **six** digits from the right side of the abacus to give 172.111512 as the correct answer.

Figure 5.18

Multiplying when the decimals have a zero integer

When either the multiplier or the multiplicand (or both) have a zero integer, for example with 0.31 only the decimal significant numbers are registered on the abacus.
Treat the numbers as integers then place the decimal point into the abacus result to get the correct answer.

Example: 0.36 x 0.02

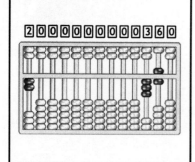

- Enter the numbers as integers, 36 x 2
- Register the MT (2) on the left side of the abacus
- Register the MD (36) on the right side of the abacus, starting at the column equal to the total number of digits, in this case column 3

Figure 5.19

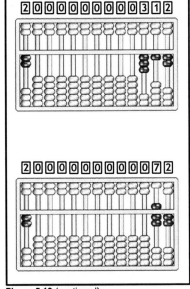

- 2nd digit of the MD is 6
- 1st digit of the MT is 2
- Base column is column 1
- 6 x 2 = 12, unregister the MD digit 6 in column 2
- Column 2 register 1
- Column 1 register 2

- 1st digit of the MD is 3
- 1st digit of the MT is 2
- Base column is column 2
- 3 x 2 = 6, unregister the MD digit 3 in column 3
- Column 2 register 6 (add it to the already registered 1)
- The abacus result is 72
- Now insert the decimal point **four** places to the left of the abacus result (0.36 **two** decimal significant figures and 0.02 also has **two** decimal significant figures), giving the correct answer as 0.0072

Figure 5.19 (continued)

Example: 0.42 x 0.003

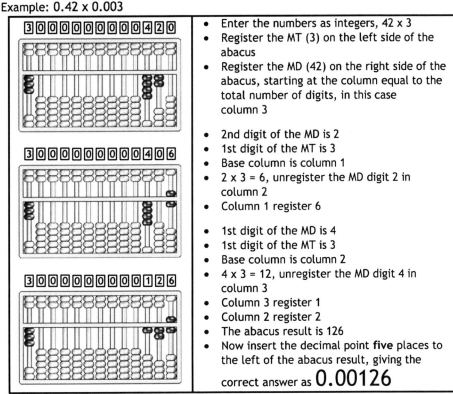

- Enter the numbers as integers, 42 x 3
- Register the MT (3) on the left side of the abacus
- Register the MD (42) on the right side of the abacus, starting at the column equal to the total number of digits, in this case column 3

- 2nd digit of the MD is 2
- 1st digit of the MT is 3
- Base column is column 1
- 2 x 3 = 6, unregister the MD digit 2 in column 2
- Column 1 register 6

- 1st digit of the MD is 4
- 1st digit of the MT is 3
- Base column is column 2
- 4 x 3 = 12, unregister the MD digit 4 in column 3
- Column 3 register 1
- Column 2 register 2
- The abacus result is 126
- Now insert the decimal point **five** places to the left of the abacus result, giving the correct answer as 0.00126

Figure 5.20

66

Example: 0.015 x 0.42

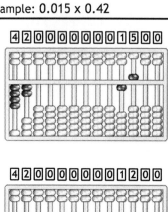

- Enter the numbers as integers, 15 x 42
- Register the MT (42) on the left side of the abacus
- Register the MD (15) on the right side of the abacus, starting at the column equal to the total number of digits, in this case column 4

The multiplying digit sequence is:

2nd 1st / 2nd 2nd **/** 1st 1st / 1st 2nd

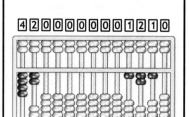

- 2nd digit of the MD is 5
- 1st digit of the MT is 4
- Base column is column 2
- 5 x 4 = 20, unregister the MD digit 5 in column 3
- Column 3 register 2
- Column 2 do nothing

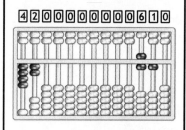

- 2nd digit of the MD is 5
- 2nd digit of the MT is 2
- Base column is column 1
- 5 x 2 = 10, nothing to unregister
- Column 2 register 1
- Column 1 do nothing

- 1st digit of the MD is 1
- 1st digit of the MT is 4
- Base column is column 3
- 1 x 4 = 4, unregister the MD digit 1 in column 4
- Column 3 register 4 (add it to the already registered 2)

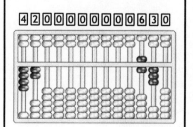

- 1st digit of the MD is 1
- 2nd digit of the MT is 2
- Base column is column 2
- 1 x 2 = 2, nothing to unregister
- Column 2 register 2 (add it to the already registered 1)
- The abacus result is 630
  Now insert the decimal point **five** places to the left of the abacus result, giving the

correct answer as 0.0063

Figure 5.21

Find the product of the following multiplications:
(see page 140 for the answers)

Number	Question
1	86 x 64
2	123 x 28
3	5426 x 24
4	236 x 153
5	23.5 x 45
6	10.895 x 1.6
7	99.1 x 0.23
8	421 x 99
9	4.32 x 0.3
10	56324 x 6

PART 6

DIVISION

Division 6

Division is the process of dividing one number by another.
The first number (the dividend), is divided by the second number (the divisor), to obtain
the result (quotient).

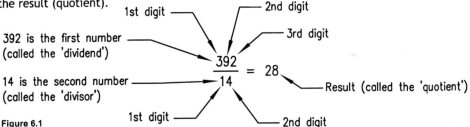

392 is the first number
(called the 'dividend')

14 is the second number
(called the 'divisor')

1st digit

2nd digit

3rd digit

$$\frac{392}{14} = 28$$

Result (called the 'quotient')

1st digit

2nd digit

Figure 6.1

On the abacus, division is slightly more complicated than performing addition, subtraction and
multiplication. It is essential to work on the correct columns on the abacus to register each
result (quotient) and when performing long division you must be able to manipulate some
numbers mentally in order to estimate how many times the divisor will divide into the
dividend.

As with multiplication, there are many different ways in which to perform division on the
abacus. The method chosen in this book involves the following:

1) To start with, place the dividend on the left side of the abacus and leave the right side
   free for your result.
2) Work by dividing digits from the left side to the right side of your dividend, in the
   example shown in figure 6.1, start with the digit 3, 9, then 2 and then any remainder
   digits.

If no decimal places are required in the answer:
Mentally simplify the numbers to get a guide as to the number of columns that will be needed
for your answer.
For example: Find 625 ÷ 14 (no decimal places required
in the answer)
Imagine 100 ÷ 10 = 10, so leave two columns for the
answer and one extra column for a decimal place (just
in the case that there is a remainder and the answer
needs to be rounded up or rounded down to create an
integer). Now, 625 ÷ 14 = 44.642 (446 in the first three
columns of the abacus), so three columns were needed
as expected, now round up the answer to 45 as no
decimal places are required in this answer.

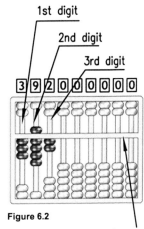

1st digit

2nd digit

3rd digit

Figure 6.2

Zero (leave this side
unregistered for the
result 'quotient')

If decimal places are required in the answer:
Add extra columns as needed.
For example: Find 625 ÷ 14 to two decimal places.
Imagine 100 ÷ 10 = 10, so two columns are needed for
the answer and a further three columns will be needed
as the answer is required to two decimal places (three
columns because the answer might have to be rounded
up or rounded down). The answer is 44.642 so round
down to 44.64 to arrive at two decimal places.

When dividing on the abacus it is also essential to know by memory the multiplication tables from 1 x 1 to 12 x 12 (see page 52) in order to help with your calculation.

Example: 253 ÷ 11 (no decimal places required in the answer)

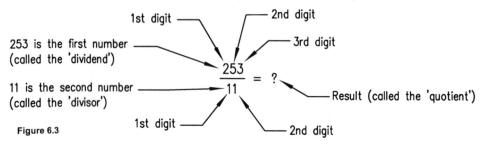

Figure 6.3

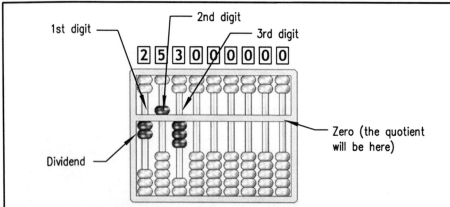

- Register the dividend 253 on the left side of the abacus and leave the right side of the abacus for the quotient
- 253 ÷ 11 so imagine 100 ÷ 10 which = 10 so we will need two columns for the answer and one column for any remainder giving a total of three columns

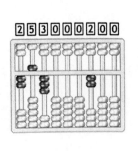

- The divisor 11 has two digits, so divide the first two digits of the dividend 25 by 11

- 11 will divide into 25, 2 times with a remainder
- Register the result 2 (in column 3) in the result area of the abacus

  Note: 253 ÷ 11, think 100 ÷ 10 = 10 which will need two columns plus one column in the case that there is a remainder. So three columns in total are required.

Figure 6.4

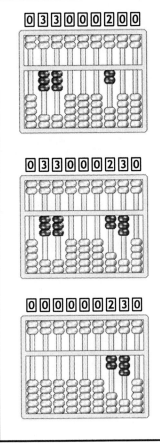

- Multiply the divisor 11 by the new result digit 2 to get 22
- Subtract this 22 from the **first two digits** of the dividend (22 of 253), this leaves 033

- The divisor is 11, so now it must be divided into the first two digits of the new dividend 33
- 11 will divide into 33, 3 times with no remainder
- Register the result 3 in the result area of the abacus in the next available column (column 2)

- Multiply the divisor 11 by the new result digit 3 to get 33
- Subtract this 33 from the **first two digits** of the new dividend 33, this leaves 0, columns 8 and 7 both become 0
- The abacus result is **23**

Figure 6.4 (continued)

Single digit dividing

Example: 86 ÷ 4 (find the answer to one decimal place)

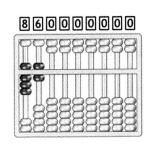

- Register the dividend 86 on the left side of the abacus and leave the right side of the abacus for the result (quotient)
- The first digit of the dividend is 8 and the first digit of the divisor is 4

Figure 6.5

74

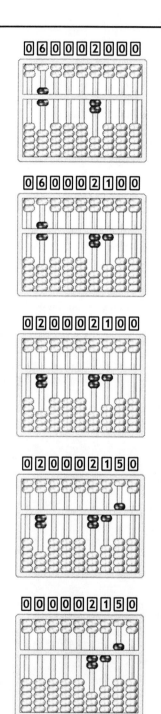

- 4 will divide into 8, 2 times
- Register the result 2 on the right side of the abacus (result area) in column 4
- Multiply the first digit of the divisor 4 by the result digit 2 to get 8
- Subtract this 8 from the first digit of the dividend (8 of 86), this leaves 06

Note: 86÷4, think 10÷1 = 10 which will need two columns. One decimal place is required in the answer, so leave two more columns for this decimal place (two because rounding up or rounding down might be required). So four columns in total are required.

- The first digit of the new dividend is 6 and the first digit of the divisor is 4
- 4 will divide into 6, 1 time with a remainder
- Register the result 1 on the right side of the abacus (result area) in the next column available (column 3)

- Multiply the first digit of the divisor 4 by the new result digit 1 to get 4
- Subtract this 4 from the new dividend (6), this leaves 2
- The first digit of the new dividend is 2 and the first digit of the divisor is 4
- 4 will not divide into 2, therefore use the next right column digit which changes the 2 to 20

- 4 will divide into 20, 5 times
- Register the result 5 in the result area of the abacus in the next column available (column 2)
- Multiply the first digit of the divisor 4 by the new result digit 5 to get 20

- Subtract this 20 from the new dividend 20, this leaves 0, columns 8 and 7 both become 0
- Now insert the decimal point into the abacus result of 215
- The abacus result is **21.5**

Figure 6.5 (continued)

Double digit dividing when the divisor is 12 or less

Example: 168 ÷ 12 (no decimal places required in the answer)

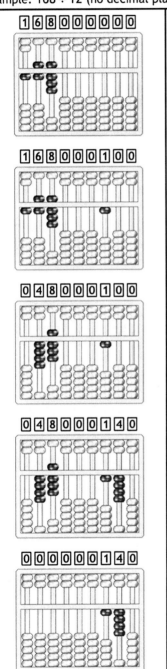

- Register the dividend 168 on the left side of the abacus and leave the right side of the abacus for the result (quotient)
- The divisor 12 has two digits, so divide the first two digits of the dividend 16 by 12

- 12 will divide into 16, 1 time with a remainder
- Register the result 1 in column 3 in the result area of the abacus

Note: 168 ÷ 12, think 100 ÷ 10 = 10 which will need two columns plus one column in the case that there is a remainder. So three columns in total are required.

- Multiply the divisor 12 by the new result digit 1 to get 12
- Subtract this 12 from the **first two digits** of the dividend (16 of 168), this leaves 048

- The divisor is 12, so now it must be divided into the first two digits of the new dividend 48
- 12 will divide into 48, 4 times with no remainder
- Register the result 4 in the result area of the abacus in the next available column (column 2)

- Multiply the divisor 12 by the new result digit 4 to get 48
- Subtract this 48 from the **first two digits** of the new dividend 48, this leaves 0, columns 8 and 7 both become 0
- The abacus result is 14

Figure 6.6

Example: 708 ÷ 12 (no decimal places required in the answer)

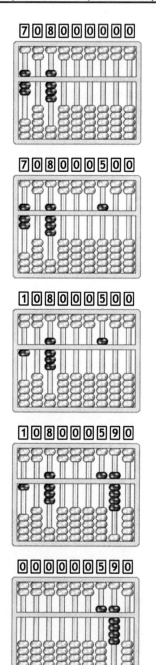

7 0 8 0 0 0 0 0

- Register the dividend 708 on the left side of the abacus and leave the right side of the abacus for the result (quotient)
- The divisor has two digits 12, so this is divided into the first two digits of the dividend 70

7 0 8 0 0 0 5 0 0

- 70 divided by 12 equals 5 with a remainder
- Register the result 5 in column 3 in the result area of the abacus

Note: 708 ÷ 12, think 100 ÷ 10 = 10 which will need two columns plus one column in the case that there is a remainder. So three columns in total are required.

1 0 8 0 0 0 5 0 0

- Multiply the divisor 12 by the new result digit 5 to get 60
- Subtract this 60 from the **first two digits** of the dividend (70 of 708), this leaves 108

1 0 8 0 0 0 5 9 0

- The divisor is 12, so now it must be divided into the first two digits of the new dividend (10 of 108)
- 12 will not divide into 10, therefore use the next right column digit which changes the 10 to 108
- 12 will divide into 108, 9 times with no remainder
- Register the result 9 in the result area of the abacus in the next available column (column 2)

0 0 0 0 0 0 5 9 0

- Multiply the divisor 12 by the new result digit 9 to get 108
- Subtract 108 from the new dividend 108, this equals 0, columns 9, 8 and 7 all become 0
- The abacus result is **59**

Figure 6.7

Double digit dividing when the divisor is greater than 12

Example: $6460 \div 76$ (no decimal places required in the answer)

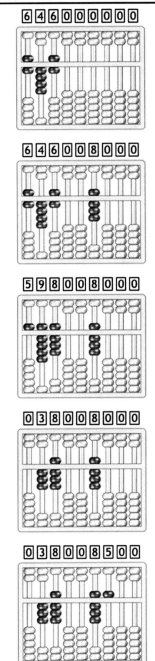

- Register the dividend 6460 on the left side of the abacus and leave the right side of the abacus for the result (quotient)

- The divisor 76 has two digits, so divide the first two digits of the dividend 64 by 76
- 76 will not divide into 64, therefore use the next right column digit which changes the 64 to 646
- 76 will divide into 646, approximately 8 times (estimate)
- Register 8 in column 4 in the result area of the abacus

Note: $6460 \div 76$, think $1000 \div 10 = 100$ which will need three columns plus one column in the case that there is a remainder. So four columns in total are required.

- Multiply the second digit of the divisor (6 of the 76) by the result digit 8 to get 48
- Subtract this 48 from the **second and third** digits of the dividend (46 of 646), this leaves 598 (use the next left column if there is not enough beads to use)

- Multiply the first digit of the divisor (7 of the 76) by the result digit 8 to get 56
- Subtract this 56 from the **first and second** digits of the new dividend (59 of the 598), this leaves 038

- The divisor 76 has two digits, so divide the first two digits of the new dividend 380 by 76
- 76 will not divide into 38, therefore use the next right column digit which changes the 38 to 380
- 76 will divide into 380, approximately 5 times (estimate)
- Register the result 5 in the result area of the abacus in the next column available (column 3)

Figure 6.8

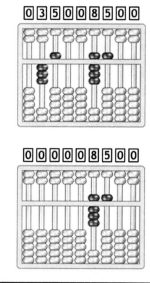

☐3☐5☐0☐0☐8☐5☐0☐0	• Multiply the second digit of the divisor (6 of the 76) by the new result digit 5 to get 30 • Subtract this 30 from the **second and third** digits of the new dividend (80 of the 380), this leaves 350
☐0☐0☐0☐0☐8☐5☐0☐0	• Multiply the first digit of the divisor (7 of the 76) by the new result digit 5 to get 35 • Subtract this 35 from the **first and second** digits of the new dividend (35 of the 350), this leaves 000, columns 8 and 7 both become 0 • The abacus result is **85**

Figure 6.8 (continued)

Triple digit dividing

Example: 33370 ÷ 142 (no decimal places required in the answer)

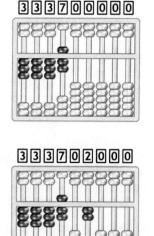

③③③⑦⓪⓪⓪⓪	• Register the dividend 33370 on the left side of the abacus and leave the right side of the abacus for the result (quotient)
③③③⑦⓪②⓪⓪	• The divisor 142 has three digits, so divide the first three digits of the dividend 333 by 142 • 142 will divide into 333, approximately 2 times (estimate) • Register 2 in column 4 in the result area of the abacus Note: 33370 ÷ 142, think 10000 ÷ 100 = 100 which will need three columns plus one column in the case that there is a remainder. So four columns in total are required.

Figure 6.9

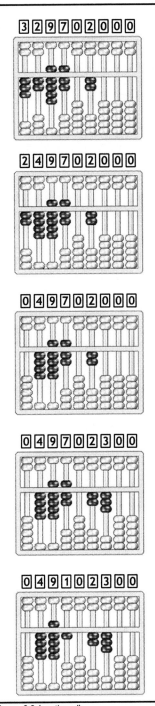

- Multiply the third digit of the divisor (2 of the 142) by the result digit 2 to get 4
- Subtract this 4 from the **third digit** of the dividend (3 of the 333), this leaves 329

(use the next left column to help)

- Multiply the second digit of the divisor (4 of the 142) by the result digit 2 to get 8
- Subtract this 8 from the **second digit** of the new dividend (2 of the 329), this leaves 249 (use the next left column to help)

- Multiply the first digit of the divisor (1 of the 142) by the result digit 2 to get 2
- Subtract this 2 from the **first digit** of the new dividend (2 of the 249), this leaves 049
- The new dividend is the next three digits 497

- 142 will divide into 497, approximately 3 times (estimate)
- Register the result 3 in the result area of the abacus in the next available column (column 3)

- Multiply the third digit of the divisor (2 of the 142) by the result digit 3 to get 6
- Subtract this 6 from the **third digit** of the new dividend (7 of the 497), this leaves 491

Figure 6.9 (continued)

80

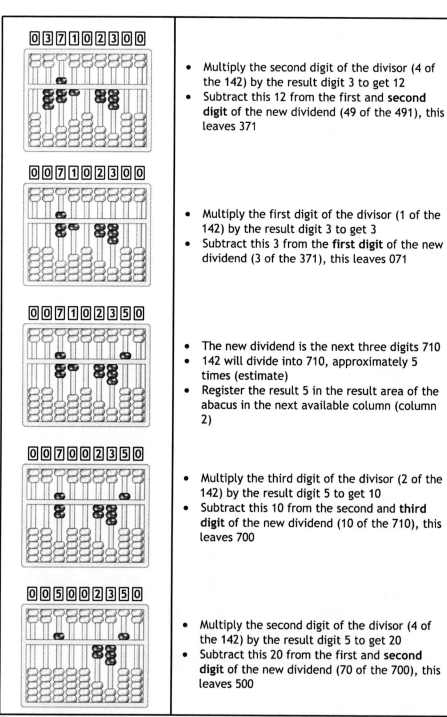

0 3 7 1 0 2 3 0 0

- Multiply the second digit of the divisor (4 of the 142) by the result digit 3 to get 12
- Subtract this 12 from the first and **second digit** of the new dividend (49 of the 491), this leaves 371

0 0 7 1 0 2 3 0 0

- Multiply the first digit of the divisor (1 of the 142) by the result digit 3 to get 3
- Subtract this 3 from the **first digit** of the new dividend (3 of the 371), this leaves 071

0 0 7 1 0 2 3 5 0

- The new dividend is the next three digits 710
- 142 will divide into 710, approximately 5 times (estimate)
- Register the result 5 in the result area of the abacus in the next available column (column 2)

0 0 7 0 0 2 3 5 0

- Multiply the third digit of the divisor (2 of the 142) by the result digit 5 to get 10
- Subtract this 10 from the second and **third digit** of the new dividend (10 of the 710), this leaves 700

0 0 5 0 0 2 3 5 0

- Multiply the second digit of the divisor (4 of the 142) by the result digit 5 to get 20
- Subtract this 20 from the first and **second digit** of the new dividend (70 of the 700), this leaves 500

Figure 6.9 (continued)

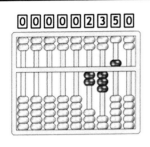

- Multiply the first digit of the divisor (1 of the 142) by the result digit 5 to get 5
- Subtract this 5 from the **first digit** of the new dividend (5 of the 500), this leaves 000
- The abacus result is **235**

Figure 6.9 (continued)

Further division examples

Example: 264 ÷ 4 (no decimal places required in the answer)

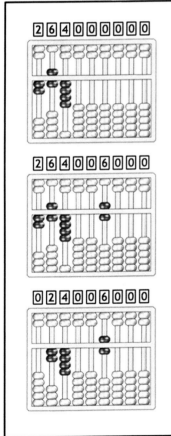

- Register the dividend 264 on the left side of the abacus

- 26 ÷ 4 = 6 with a remainder
- Register 6 in the results column

- 6 x 4 = 24
- Subtract 24 from 26, this leaves 02 (columns 9 and 8)

Figure 6.10

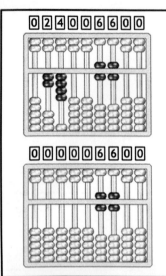

- 24 ÷ 4 = 6
- Register 6 in the results column

- 6 x 4 = 24
- 24 - 24 = 0, no remainder
- The abacus result is **66**

Figure 6.10 (continued)

Example: **192 ÷ 8** (no decimal places required in the answer)

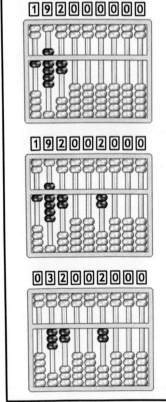

- Register the dividend 192 on the left side of the abacus

- 19 ÷ 8 = 2 with a remainder
- Register 2 in the results column

- 2 x 8 = 16
- Subtract 16 from 19, this leaves 03 (columns 9 and 8)

Figure 6.11

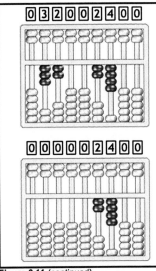

- $32 \div 8 = 4$
- Register 4 in the results column

- $4 \times 8 = 32$
- $32 - 32 = 0$, no remainder
- The abacus result is **24**

Figure 6.11 (continued)

A thirteen column abacus will be used in the following examples

Example: $185 \div 7$ (find the result to one decimal place)

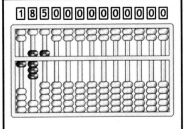

- Register the dividend 185 on the left side of the abacus

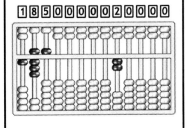

- $18 \div 7 = 2$ with a remainder
- Register 2 in the results column

  Note: $185 \div 7$, think $100 \div 1 = 100$ which will need three columns plus two columns as one decimal place is required in the answer. So five columns in total are required.

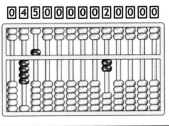

- $2 \times 7 = 14$
- Subtract 14 from 18, this leaves 04 (columns 13 and 12)

Figure 6.12

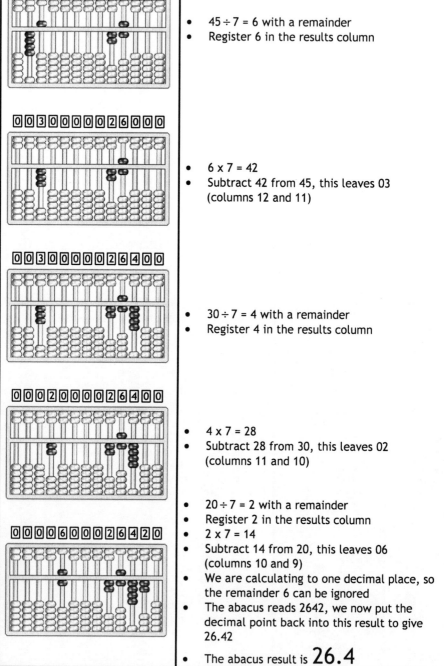

84

045000002 6000

- 45 ÷ 7 = 6 with a remainder
- Register 6 in the results column

003000002 6000

- 6 x 7 = 42
- Subtract 42 from 45, this leaves 03 (columns 12 and 11)

003000002 6400

- 30 ÷ 7 = 4 with a remainder
- Register 4 in the results column

000200002 6400

- 4 x 7 = 28
- Subtract 28 from 30, this leaves 02 (columns 11 and 10)

000060002 6420

- 20 ÷ 7 = 2 with a remainder
- Register 2 in the results column
- 2 x 7 = 14
- Subtract 14 from 20, this leaves 06 (columns 10 and 9)
- We are calculating to one decimal place, so the remainder 6 can be ignored
- The abacus reads 2642, we now put the decimal point back into this result to give 26.42
- The abacus result is **26.4**

Figure 6.12 (continued)

Example: $384 \div 16$ (no decimal places required in the answer)

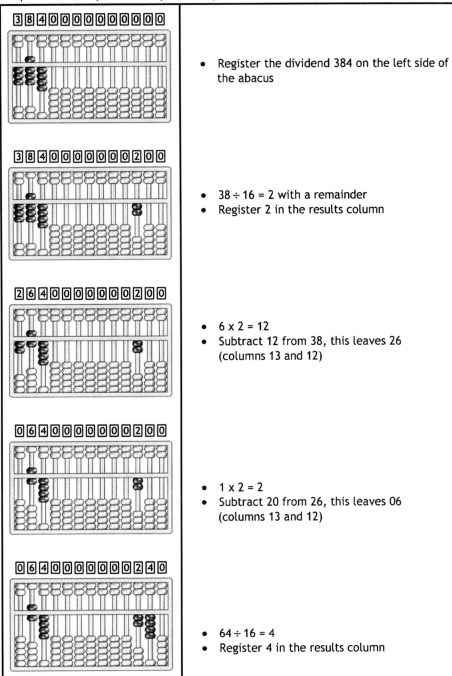

- Register the dividend 384 on the left side of the abacus

- $38 \div 16 = 2$ with a remainder
- Register 2 in the results column

- $6 \times 2 = 12$
- Subtract 12 from 38, this leaves 26 (columns 13 and 12)

- $1 \times 2 = 2$
- Subtract 20 from 26, this leaves 06 (columns 13 and 12)

- $64 \div 16 = 4$
- Register 4 in the results column

Figure 6.13

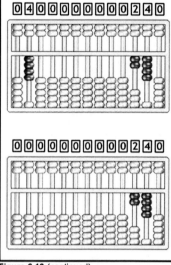

- 6 x 4 = 24
- Subtract 24 from 64, this leaves 40 (columns 12 and 11)

- 1 x 4 = 4, now 40 - 40 = 0, unregister 40
- The abacus result is **24**

Figure 6.13 (continued)

Example: $463 \div 16$ (find the result to two decimal places)

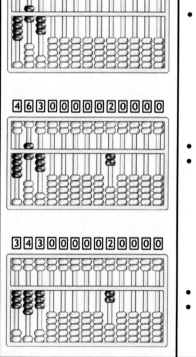

- Register the dividend 463 on the left side of the abacus

- $46 \div 16 = 2$ with a remainder
- Register 2 in the results column

- 6 x 2 = 12
- Subtract 12 from 46, this leaves 34 (columns 13 and 12)

Figure 6.14

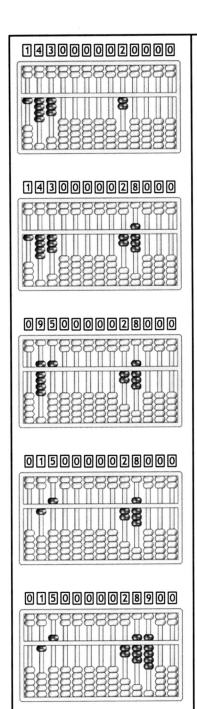

- 1 x 2 = 2
- Subtract 20 from 34, this leaves 14 (columns 13 and 12)

- 143 ÷ 16 = 8 (estimate)
  If required you can use the empty columns in the middle of the abacus to multiply 16 x 8 to check your estimate. Remember to unregister these columns afterwards.
- Register 8 in the results column

- 6 x 8 = 48
- Subtract 48 from 143, this leaves 095 (columns 13, 12 and 11)

- 1 x 8 = 8
- Subtract 80 from 95, this leaves 15 (columns 12 and 11)

- 150 ÷ 16 = 9 (estimate)
- Register 9 in the results column

Figure 6.14 (continued)

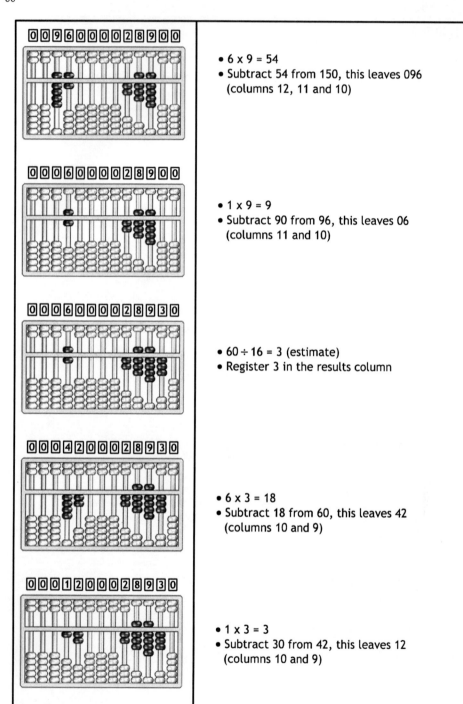

- 6 x 9 = 54
- Subtract 54 from 150, this leaves 096 (columns 12, 11 and 10)

- 1 x 9 = 9
- Subtract 90 from 96, this leaves 06 (columns 11 and 10)

- 60 ÷ 16 = 3 (estimate)
- Register 3 in the results column

- 6 x 3 = 18
- Subtract 18 from 60, this leaves 42 (columns 10 and 9)

- 1 x 3 = 3
- Subtract 30 from 42, this leaves 12 (columns 10 and 9)

Figure 6.14 (continued)

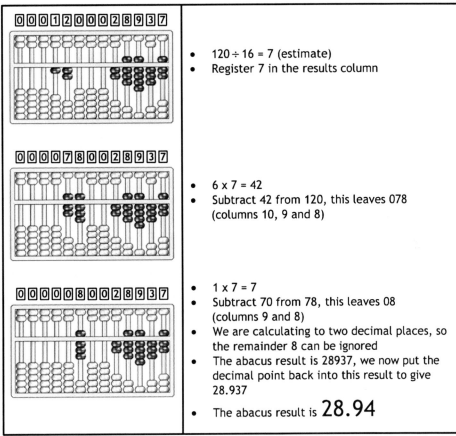

`0 0 0 1 2 0 0 0 2 8 9 3 7`	• $120 \div 16 = 7$ (estimate) • Register 7 in the results column
`0 0 0 0 7 8 0 0 2 8 9 3 7`	• $6 \times 7 = 42$ • Subtract 42 from 120, this leaves 078 (columns 10, 9 and 8)
`0 0 0 0 0 8 0 0 2 8 9 3 7`	• $1 \times 7 = 7$ • Subtract 70 from 78, this leaves 08 (columns 9 and 8) • We are calculating to two decimal places, so the remainder 8 can be ignored • The abacus result is 28937, we now put the decimal point back into this result to give 28.937 • The abacus result is **28.94**

Figure 6.14 (continued)

Example: $5136 \div 321$ (no decimal places are required in the answer)

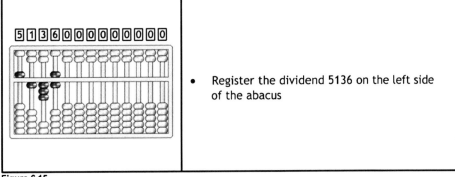

`5 1 3 6 0 0 0 0 0 0 0 0 0`	• Register the dividend 5136 on the left side of the abacus

Figure 6.15

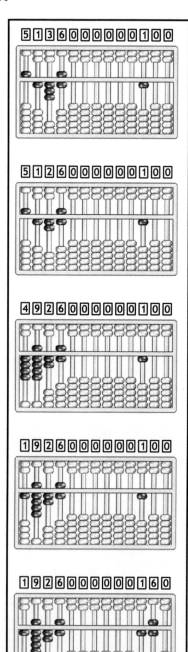

- 513 ÷ 321 = 1 with a remainder
- Register 1 in the results column

- 1 x 1 = 1
- Subtract 1 from 513, this leaves 512 (columns 13, 12 and 11)

- 2 x 1 = 2
- Subtract 20 from 512, this leaves 492 (columns 13, 12 and 11)

- 3 x 1 = 3
- Subtract 300 from 492, this leaves 192 (columns 13, 12 and 11)

- 1926 ÷ 321 = 6 (estimate)
  (7 x 300 = 2100 but 6 x 300 = 1800)

- Register 6 in the results column

Figure 6.15 (continued)

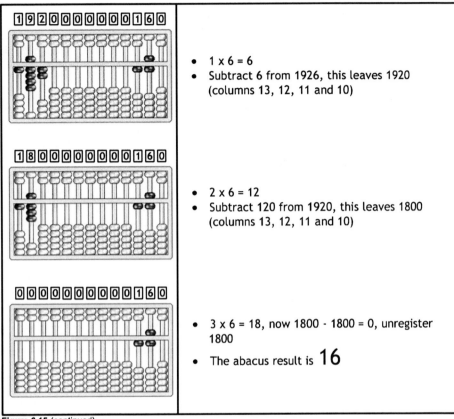

- 1 x 6 = 6
- Subtract 6 from 1926, this leaves 1920 (columns 13, 12, 11 and 10)

- 2 x 6 = 12
- Subtract 120 from 1920, this leaves 1800 (columns 13, 12, 11 and 10)

- 3 x 6 = 18, now 1800 - 1800 = 0, unregister 1800
- The abacus result is **16**

Figure 6.15 (continued)

Dividing numbers that contain decimals

When you have to divide numbers that contain decimals, it is best to convert the decimals to integers, then make the calculation on the abacus.

When there is a decimal point, either in the divisor or the dividend, you must always be consistent and move the decimal point the same number of places for both of the numbers.

Note:

$$8000 \div 250 = 800 \div 25 = 80 \div 2.5 = 8 \div 0.25 = 0.8 \div 0.025 = 0.08 \div 0.0025$$

Examples:

$624 \div 2.6 = 240$

To make the decimal divisor (2.6) an integer, the decimal point must be moved one place to the right, therefore the dividend (624) must also have its decimal point moved one place to the right.

$$624 \div 2.6 = 6240 \div 26$$

The calculation $6240 \div 26$ can now be done on the abacus to get the same result of 240.

Some examples:

Example	Move the decimal point	Calculation to perform on the abacus	Result on the abacus
$7.35 \div 21 = 0.35$	$7.35 \div 21 = 0.35$ 2 places 2 places	$735 \div 2100$	0.35
$3.24 \div 0.006 = 540$	$3.24 \div 0.006 = 540$ 3 places 3 places	$3240 \div 6$	540
$88 \div 0.4 = 220$	$88 \div 0.4 = 220$ 1 place 1 place	$880 \div 4$	220

Table 6.1

Note:
From the examples shown in table 6.1, it can be seen that the decimal point must be moved the same number of places in the dividend as in the divisor i.e. if you move the decimal point three places in the dividend the decimal point must be moved three places in the divisor also.

Placing of the decimal point in your answer.

When placing the decimal point in your answer it is important to look at the numbers in the calculation that you are performing and then to be able to judge the placing of the decimal point in the answer. Look at the examples in table 6.2 to see a pattern.

Sometimes a quick way to find the decimal point position is to move the decimal point in both the dividend and the divisor.

Example:

$$0.1 \div 10 = 1 \div 100 = 0.01$$

÷ by 0.1	÷ by 1	÷ by 10	÷ by 100
$\dfrac{0.001}{0.1} = 0.01$	$\dfrac{0.001}{1} = 0.001$	$\dfrac{0.001}{10} = 0.0001$	$\dfrac{0.001}{100} = 0.00001$
$\dfrac{0.01}{0.1} = 0.1$	$\dfrac{0.01}{1} = 0.01$	$\dfrac{0.01}{10} = 0.001$	$\dfrac{0.01}{100} = 0.0001$
$\dfrac{0.1}{0.1} = 1$	$\dfrac{0.1}{1} = 0.1$	$\dfrac{0.1}{10} = 0.01$	$\dfrac{0.1}{100} = 0.001$
$\dfrac{1}{0.1} = 10$	$\dfrac{1}{1} = 1$	$\dfrac{1}{10} = 0.1$	$\dfrac{1}{100} = 0.01$
$\dfrac{10}{0.1} = 100$	$\dfrac{10}{1} = 10$	$\dfrac{10}{10} = 1$	$\dfrac{10}{100} = 0.1$
$\dfrac{100}{0.1} = 1000$	$\dfrac{100}{1} = 100$	$\dfrac{100}{10} = 10$	$\dfrac{100}{100} = 1$
$\dfrac{1000}{0.1} = 10000$	$\dfrac{1000}{1} = 1000$	$\dfrac{1000}{10} = 100$	$\dfrac{1000}{100} = 10$
$\dfrac{10000}{0.1} = 100000$	$\dfrac{10000}{1} = 10000$	$\dfrac{10000}{10} = 1000$	$\dfrac{10000}{100} = 100$

Table 6.2

If you become familiar with table 6.2, you can use this knowledge to make a good estimate of the answer to your calculation.

Example:
If you have a calculation to perform like 6888 ÷ 123, imagine the number in a simpler form, so 6888 becomes 7000 and 123 becomes 100, so 7000 ÷ 100 = 70, so when 6888 ÷ 123 gives the result on the abacus shown here,

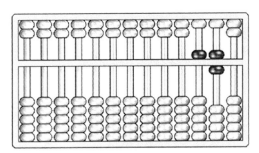

Figure 6.16

you then know that 5.6 is too small and 560 is too large so 56 must be the correct answer.

Some examples

Your calculation	Imagine	Abacus result	Where should the decimal point be?	Correct result
$1472 \div 23$	$1400 \div 20$		Compare 70 to 6.4, 64 or 640 64 is the closest to 70	64
$806.4 \div 22.4$	$800 \div 20$		Compare 40 to 3.6, 36 or 360 36 is the closest to 40	36
$16.83 \div 0.9$	$20 \div 1$		Compare 20 to 1.87, 18.7 or 187 18.7 is the closest to 20	18.7
$7.5 \div 0.025$	$8 \div 0.02 = 800 \div 2$		Compare 400 to 3, 30, 300 or 3000 300 is the closest to 400	300

Table 6.3

uestions | **Find the answer by estimating the result:**
(see page 141 for the answers)

No.	Question	Place a tick in the box containing the correct answer				
1	$\dfrac{360}{9}$	0.04 ☐	0.4 ☐	4 ☐	40 ☐	400 ☐
2	$\dfrac{392}{9.8}$	0.04 ☐	0.4 ☐	4 ☐	40 ☐	400 ☐
3	$\dfrac{207.9}{2.1}$	0.099 ☐	0.99 ☐	9.9 ☐	99 ☐	990 ☐
4	$\dfrac{46.8}{0.9}$	0.052 ☐	0.52 ☐	5.2 ☐	52 ☐	520 ☐
5	$\dfrac{0.03}{0.001}$	0.03 ☐	0.3 ☐	3 ☐	30 ☐	300 ☐
6	$\dfrac{0.0008}{0.0002}$	0.04 ☐	0.4 ☐	4 ☐	40 ☐	400 ☐
7	$\dfrac{0.8}{0.002}$	0.04 ☐	0.4 ☐	4 ☐	40 ☐	400 ☐
8	$\dfrac{0.315}{0.9}$	0.035 ☐	0.35 ☐	3.5 ☐	35 ☐	350 ☐

 uestions | **Find the quotient for the following divisions:**
(see page 141 for the answers)

Number	Question
9	32 ÷ 4
10	672 ÷ 12
11	576 ÷ 24
12	1995.2 ÷ 46.4
13	44 ÷ 2.2

Number	Question
14	0.08 ÷ 0.002
15	4680 ÷ 20
16	653.4 ÷ 9.9
17	0.0072 ÷ 0.0006
18	5676 ÷ 11

PART 7

EXTRA BEAD

Extra bead 7

Using the extra bead method

Old Chinese methods of using an abacus involved using both beads above the beam and all beads below the beam.

Both beads above the beam have a value of 5 units each so both beads touching the beam (registered) would register a total of 10 units (see figure 7.1). When all beads below the beam are touching the the beam (registered) this would register a total of 5 units (1 unit for each bead).

Another old Chinese method was to use the suspended bead, meaning that the top most bead above the beam would lie halfway down the rod, neither touching the registered bead below it or touching the top of the frame (see figure 7.3), this suspended bead has a value of 10 units on its own.

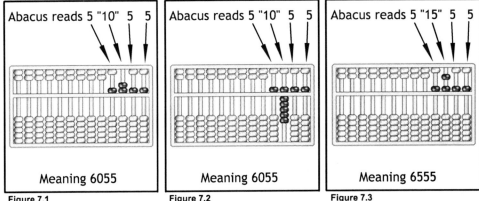

Abacus reads 5 "10" 5 5	Abacus reads 5 "10" 5 5	Abacus reads 5 "15" 5 5
Meaning 6055	Meaning 6055	Meaning 6555
Figure 7.1	Figure 7.2	Figure 7.3

Multiplication using the extra bead

Note:
This old method involves using a different order in which the digits are multiplied together, compared to the more modern techniques.

Extra bead method example: 589 x 492

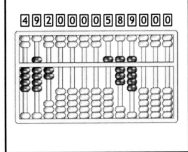

- Register the multiplicand (MD) 589 on the right side of the abacus, columns 6, 5 and 4 and leave three columns unregistered, columns 3, 2 and 1 (use a total of six columns because the multiplicand has three digits and the multiplier (MT) has three digits giving a total of six)

- Register the multiplier 492 on the left side of the abacus.

Figure 7.4

The multiplier sequence is as follows:

Start with this:	Followed by:	Followed by:
• 1st = 9 x 9	• 1st = 8 x 9	• 1st = 5 x 9
• 2nd = 9 x 2	• 2nd = 8 x 2	• 2nd = 5 x 2
• 3rd = 9 x 4	• 3rd = 8 x 4	• 3rd = 5 x 4
MDxMT	MDxMT	MDxMT

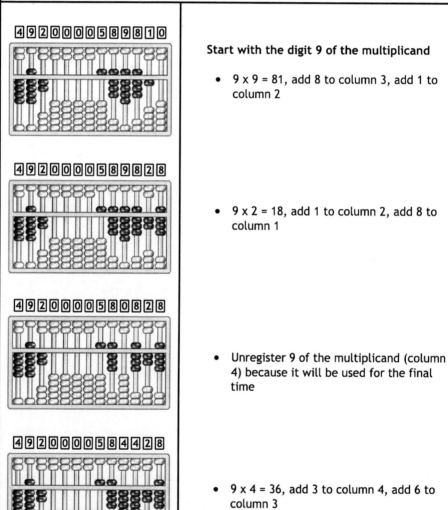

Start with the digit 9 of the multiplicand

- 9 x 9 = 81, add 8 to column 3, add 1 to column 2

- 9 x 2 = 18, add 1 to column 2, add 8 to column 1

- Unregister 9 of the multiplicand (column 4) because it will be used for the final time

- 9 x 4 = 36, add 3 to column 4, add 6 to column 3

Figure 7.4 (continued)

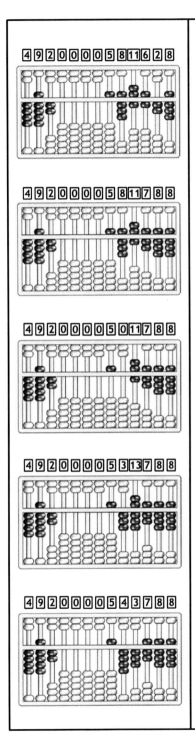

Next use digit 8 of the multiplicand

- 8 x 9 = 72, add 7 to column 4, add 2 to column 3
- Because we are using digit 8 of the multiplicand, use the extra bead to make '11' (7 + 4) so as not to disturb the 8 bead in column 5 as this could cause confusion

- 8 x 2 = 16, add 1 to column 3, add 6 to column 2

- Unregister 8 of the multiplicand (column 5) because it will be used for the final time

- 8 x 4 = 32, add 3 to column 5, add 2 to column 4

- Clear the 13 on column 4 by adding 1 to column 5 and leaving 3 on column 4

Figure 7.4 (continued)

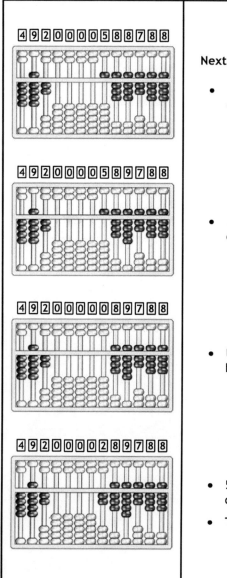

Next use digit 5 of the multiplicand

- 5 x 9 = 45, add 4 to column 5, add 5 to column 4

- 5 x 2 = 10, add 1 to column 4, add 0 to column 3

- Unregister 5 of the multiplicand (column 6) because it will be used for the final time

- 5 x 4 = 20, add 2 to column 6, add 0 to column 5
- The abacus result is **289788**

Figure 7.4 (continued)

Multiplication using the suspended bead method

When multiplying digits, sometimes there will be a case where one column's result is 15 or larger, then the suspended bead method can be used.

Suspended bead method example: 989 x 998

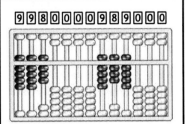

- Register the multiplicand 989 on the right side of the abacus, columns 6, 5 and 4 and leave three columns unregistered, columns 3, 2 and 1 (use a total of six columns because the multiplicand has three digits and the multiplier has three digits giving a total of six).
- Register the multiplier 998 on the left side of the abacus.

The multiplier sequence is as follows:

First this:	Followed by:	Followed by:
• 1st = 9 x 9	• 1st = 8 x 9	• 1st = 9 x 9
• 2nd = 9 x 8	• 2nd = 8 x 8	• 2nd = 9 x 8
• 3rd = 9 x 9	• 3rd = 8 x 9	• 3rd = 9 x 9
MDxMT	MDxMT	MDxMT

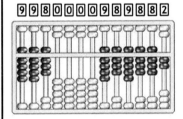

Start with the digit 9 of the multiplicand

- 9 x 9 = 81, add 8 to column 3, add 1 to column 2

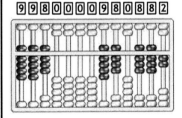

- 9 x 8 = 72, add 7 to column 2, add 2 to column 1

- Unregister 9 of the multiplicand (column 4) because it will be used for the final time

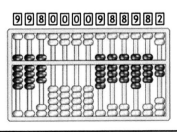

- 9 x 9 = 81, add 8 to column 4, add 1 to column 3

Figure 7.5

104

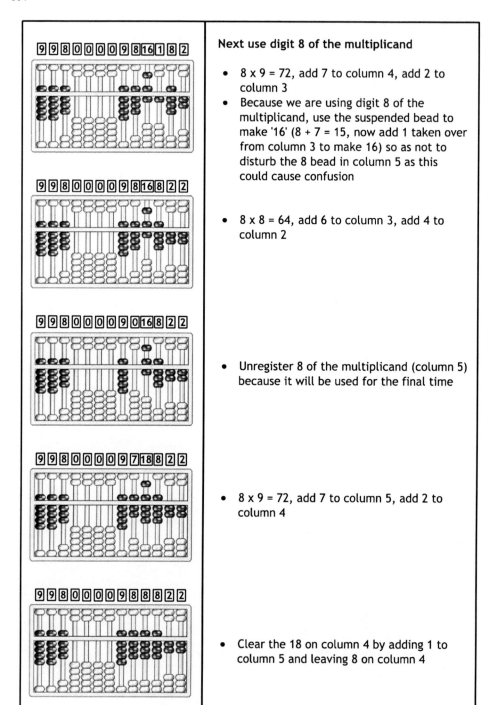

Next use digit 8 of the multiplicand

- 8 x 9 = 72, add 7 to column 4, add 2 to column 3
- Because we are using digit 8 of the multiplicand, use the suspended bead to make '16' (8 + 7 = 15, now add 1 taken over from column 3 to make 16) so as not to disturb the 8 bead in column 5 as this could cause confusion

- 8 x 8 = 64, add 6 to column 3, add 4 to column 2

- Unregister 8 of the multiplicand (column 5) because it will be used for the final time

- 8 x 9 = 72, add 7 to column 5, add 2 to column 4

- Clear the 18 on column 4 by adding 1 to column 5 and leaving 8 on column 4

Figure 7.5 (continued)

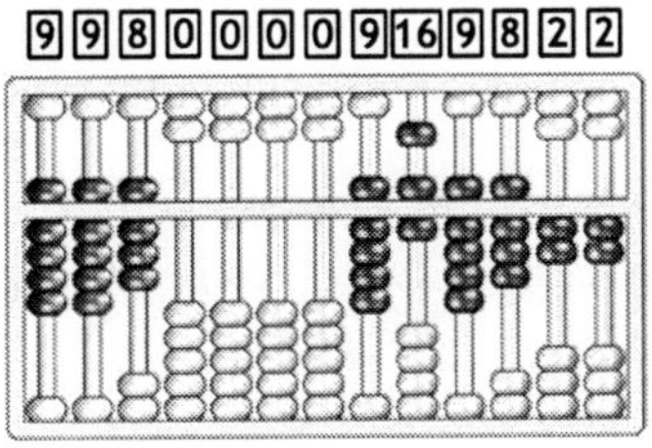

9 9 8 0 0 0 0 9 16 9 8 2 2

Next use digit 9 of the multiplicand

- 9 x 9 = 81, add 8 to column 5, add 1 to column 4

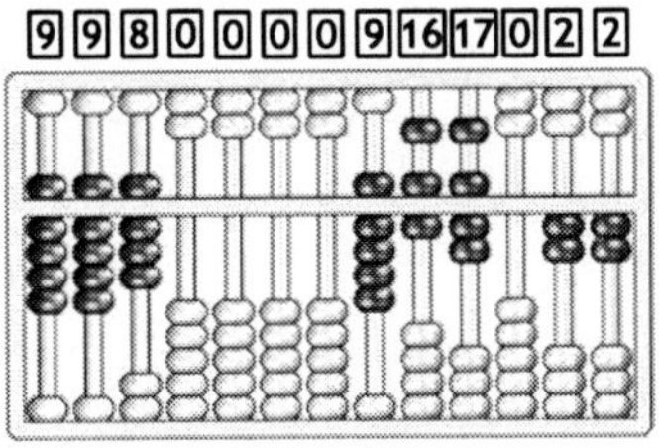

9 9 8 0 0 0 0 9 16 17 0 2 2

- 9 x 8 = 72, add 7 to column 4, add 2 to column 3

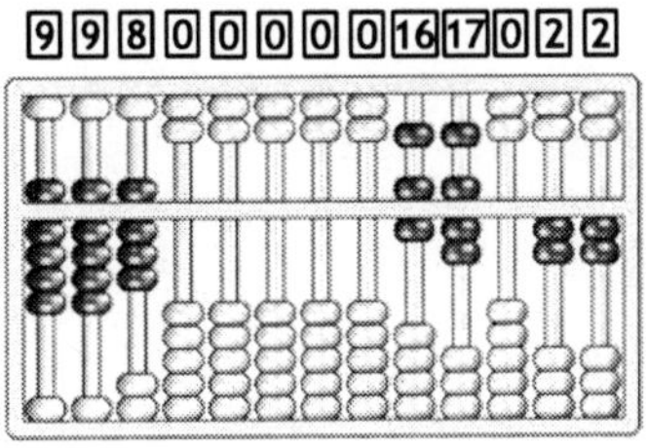

9 9 8 0 0 0 0 0 16 17 0 2 2

- Unregister 9 of the multiplicand (column 6) because it will be used for the final time

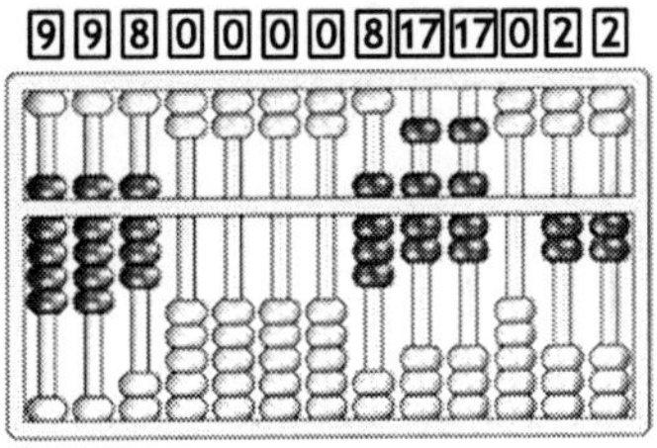

9 9 8 0 0 0 0 8 17 17 0 2 2

- 9 x 9 = 81, add 8 to column 6, add 1 to column 5

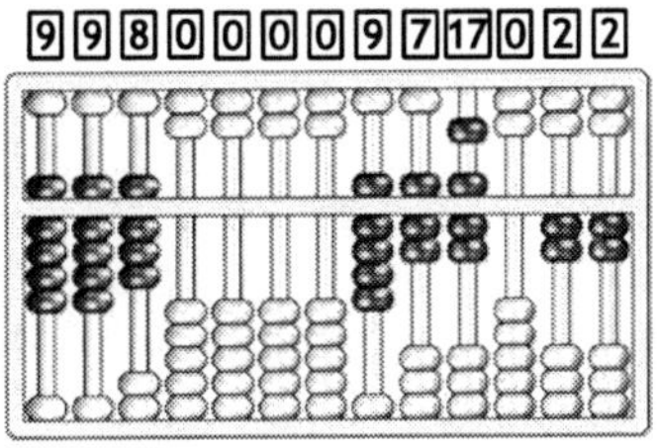

9 9 8 0 0 0 0 9 7 17 0 2 2

- Clear the 17 on column 5 by adding 1 to column 6 and leaving 7 on column 5

Figure 7.5 (continued)

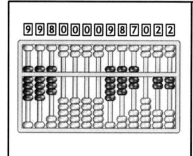

- Clear the 17 on column 4 by adding 1 to column 5 and leaving 7 on column 4
- The abacus result is **987022**

Figure 7.5 (continued)

Division using the extra bead method

Example: 387 ÷ 9

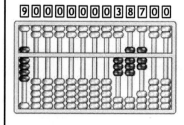

- Register the dividend 387 on the right side of the abacus, columns 5, 4 and 3 and leave two columns unregistered, columns 2 and 1 for remainders (the quotient will replace the digits of the dividend during the calculation)
- Place the divisor 9 on the left side of the abacus

First use the 3 from column 5

- 9 will not divide into 3, so mentally change 3 to 30, think of 30 ÷ 9 which divides 3 times with a remainder of 3
- Unregister 3 in column 5

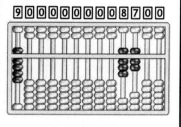

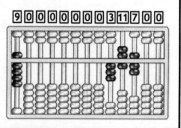

- Add the result 3 (from 30 ÷ 9) to column 5
- Add the remainder 3 (from 30 ÷ 9) to column 4, use the extra bead to make 11 (from 3 + 8)

Figure 7.6

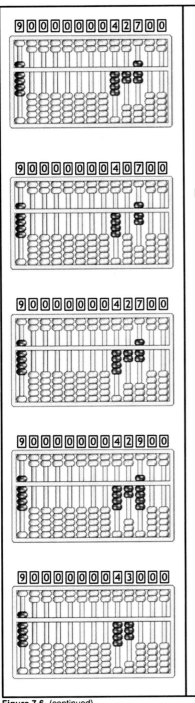

- 11 is greater than 9 (the divisor), to clear this 11 we minus 9 from column 4 (presently 11) and add 1 to column 5, leave the remainder 2 in column 4

Now use the 2 from column 4

- 9 will not divide into 2, so mentally change 2 to 20, think of 20 ÷ 9 which divides 2 times with a remainder of 2
- Unregister 2 in column 4

- Add the result 2 (from 20 ÷ 9) to column 4

- Add the remainder 2 (from 20 ÷ 9) to column 3

Now use the 9 from column 3

- 9 will divide into 9, 1 time
- Unregister digit 9 in column 3
- Add the result 1 (from 9 ÷ 9) to column 4 (note, this time we do not place the result in column 3 as 9 could divide into 9 without increasing it by a power of ten i.e. from 9 to 90)
- The abacus result is 43

Figure 7.6 (continued)

Division using the suspended bead method

When dividing digits, sometimes there will be a case where one column's result is 15 or larger, then the suspended bead method can be used.

Example: 882 ÷ 9

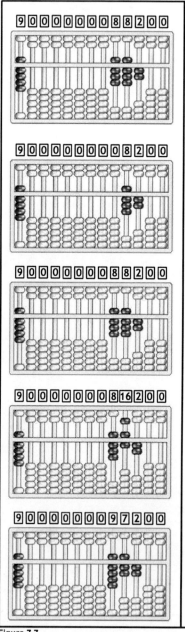

- Register the dividend 882 on the right side of the abacus, columns 5, 4 and 3 and leave two columns unregistered, columns 2 and 1 for remainders (the quotient will replace the digits of the dividend during the calculation)
- Place the divisor 9 on the left side of the abacus

First use the 8 from column 5

- 9 will not divide into 8, so mentally change 8 to 80, think of 80 ÷ 9 which divides 8 times with a remainder of 8
- Unregister 8 in column 5

- Add the result 8 (from 80 ÷ 9) to column 5

- Add the remainder 8 (from 80 ÷ 9) to column 4, use the suspended bead to make 16 (from 8 + 8)

- 16 is greater than 9 (the divisor), to clear this 16 we minus 9 from column 4 (presently 16) and add 1 to column 5, leave the remainder 7 in column 4

Figure 7.7

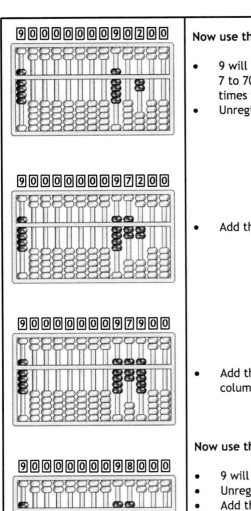

Now use the 7 from column 4

- 9 will not divide into 7, so mentally change 7 to 70, think of 70 ÷ 9 which divides 7 times with a remainder of 7
- Unregister 7 in column 4

- Add the result 7 (from 70 ÷ 9) to column 4

- Add the remainder 7 (from 80 ÷ 9) to column 3

Now use the 9 from column 3

- 9 will divide into 9, 1 time
- Unregister 9 in column 3
- Add the result 1 (from 9 ÷ 9) to column 4 (note, this time we do not place the result in column 3 as 9 could divide into 9 without increasing it by a power of ten i.e. from 9 to 90)
- The abacus result is **98**

Figure 7.7 (continued)

PART 8

SQUARE ROOTS

Square roots 8

Finding square roots on an abacus is similar to the method used when calculating it on paper.

The square root symbol is $\sqrt{}$ (also known as the radical).

Numbers that have square roots have a positive and negative one, i.e. $3^2 = 3 \times 3 = 9$ but also $(-3)^2 = -3 \times -3 = 9$. In this chapter we deal with positive roots only.

The **square of a number** is the number multiplied by itself i.e. the square of $4 = 4 \times 4 = 4^2 = 16$, the square of $5 = 5 \times 5 = 5^2 = 25$ etc.

The **square root of a given number** is a number that when multiplied by itself gives that given number.
i.e. $\sqrt{16} = 4$ (meaning the square root of 16 equals 4) because $4 \times 4 = 16$
(Note: The square root of 16 is also -4 because $-4 \times -4 = 16$).

A whole number multiplied by itself will give what is known as a 'Perfect square'. Table 8.1 shows some examples of 'Number squared', 'Perfect square' and 'Square roots' for whole numbers from 1 to 10.

Number	Number squared = Perfect square	Square root = Number
1	$1^2 = 1$	$\sqrt{1} = 1$
2	$2^2 = 4$	$\sqrt{4} = 2$
3	$3^2 = 9$	$\sqrt{9} = 3$
4	$4^2 = 16$	$\sqrt{16} = 4$
5	$5^2 = 25$	$\sqrt{25} = 5$
6	$6^2 = 36$	$\sqrt{36} = 6$
7	$7^2 = 49$	$\sqrt{49} = 7$
8	$8^2 = 64$	$\sqrt{64} = 8$
9	$9^2 = 81$	$\sqrt{81} = 9$
10	$10^2 = 100$	$\sqrt{100} = 10$

Table 8.1

The perfect squares are the squares of the whole numbers i.e. 1, 4, 9, 16, 25, 36, 49, 64, 81, 100....etc.

Finding the square root of numbers that are or aren't perfect squares, can be easily done on an abacus with some practice. To refresh your memory, here is one example of how to perform a square root calculation by the manual method on paper.

Example: Find the $\sqrt{1225}$

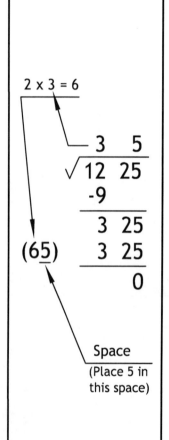

	• Firstly, separate the number into two digit numbers, starting at the decimal point with a space between each pair of numbers (1225.0) e.g. $\sqrt{12\ 25}$ Start at the decimal point
	Note, if the number was 136.74 the pair separation would be $\sqrt{1\ 36\ 74}$
$2 \times 3 = 6$	• Look at the left most pair (sometimes a single digit number) in this case 12 and find the largest number whose square is less than or equal to it $4^2 = 16$ this is too big $3^2 = 9$ this is good
$\sqrt{\begin{matrix}3\ \ \ \ 5\\ 12\ \ 25\end{matrix}}$ -9	• Place the result 3 above the 12 and above the radical sign
3 25 (65) 3 25	• Place the square of 3, which is 9, below the number 12 and subtract
0	• Bring down the next two digit number (25) to create 325
	• Multiply the result 3 by 2 and place the result 6 in brackets with a space on the right side of it
Space (Place 5 in this space)	• Find the largest number that when placed in this space and multiplied by this number will be less than or equal to 325. i.e. **64 x 4 = 256** this is too small **66 x 6 = 396** this is too big **65 x 5 = 325** this is good Place 5 in the space
	• Place the result 5 above the next two digit number 25 and above the radical sign, then subtract the result 325 from 325, this gives zero.
	• The $\sqrt{1225}$ is **35**

Figure 8.1

Finding square roots on the abacus

The abacus should be separated into three areas:

1) The right side for the answer (result area) the amount of columns left for decimals depends on the accuracy of the answer required.
2) Middle of the abacus for temporary calculations (temporary area)
3) The left area is to register the number that you are finding the root of (work area).

Note: A larger abacus (13 columns or more) would be needed to find the root of larger numbers.

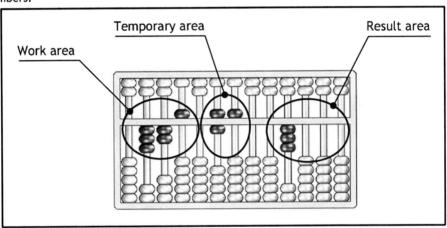

Figure 8.2

Example: Find the √ 1225

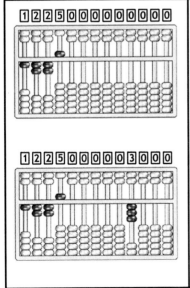

- Register 1225 on the left side of the abacus
- When 1225 is split into two digit numbers (12 25) the first two digit number is 12

- The largest perfect square that is less than or equal to 12 is 3, because $3^2 = 9$

- Register 3 on the right side of the abacus (result area) in column 4

Note: Count the number of digits in the number that you are finding the square root of.

In this case √ 1225 has four digits, so start to register the result in column 4. If decimal places are required in the answer, then leave more columns for the result.

Figure 8.3

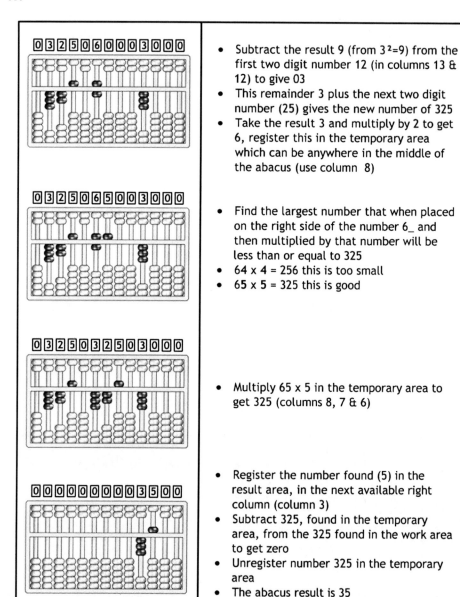

`0 3 2 5 0 6 0 0 3 0 0 0`

- Subtract the result 9 (from 3^2=9) from the first two digit number 12 (in columns 13 & 12) to give 03
- This remainder 3 plus the next two digit number (25) gives the new number of 325
- Take the result 3 and multiply by 2 to get 6, register this in the temporary area which can be anywhere in the middle of the abacus (use column 8)

`0 3 2 5 0 6 5 0 0 3 0 0 0`

- Find the largest number that when placed on the right side of the number 6_ and then multiplied by that number will be less than or equal to 325
- 64 x 4 = 256 this is too small
- 65 x 5 = 325 this is good

`0 3 2 5 0 3 2 5 0 3 0 0 0`

- Multiply 65 x 5 in the temporary area to get 325 (columns 8, 7 & 6)

`0 0 0 0 0 0 0 0 3 5 0 0`

- Register the number found (5) in the result area, in the next available right column (column 3)
- Subtract 325, found in the temporary area, from the 325 found in the work area to get zero
- Unregister number 325 in the temporary area
- The abacus result is 35
- The √ 1225 is 35

Figure 8.3 (continued)

117

Example: Find the √ 1.44 (find the answer to one decimal place)

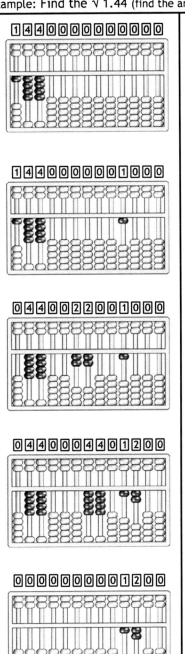

- Mentally separate the number 1.44 into two digit numbers starting at the decimal point to get 1 44
- Register 144 in the work area of the abacus

  Note: Start to register the result in column 4, three columns for the digits of 144 and one column for the decimal point.

- Use the first two digit number, in this case it is only a single digit (number 1)
- The largest perfect square that is less than or equal to 1 is 1, because $1^2 = 1$
- Register 1 in the result area of the abacus

- Subtract 1 (from $1^2 = 1$) from the work area of the abacus (number 1 in column 13)
- Use the next two digit number (44) to create the next working number which will be 44
- Use the temporary area to calculate the next number. Multiply the result 1 by 2 to get 2 and register this in the temporary area (column 8)
- Find the largest number that when placed on the right side of the number 2_ and then multiplied by itself will be less than or equal to 44
- 22 x 2 = 44 this is good, so register the result 2 in the result area of the abacus (column 3)

- Subtract the temporary number 44 from the working number 44 to get zero
- Unregister the temporary number 44
- The abacus result is 12, put the decimal point back into this number to get 1.2
- The √ 1.44 is **1.2**

Figure 8.4

118

Further examples: (A seventeen column abacus will be used for the next two examples)

Example: Find the √ 34 (find the answer to one decimal place)

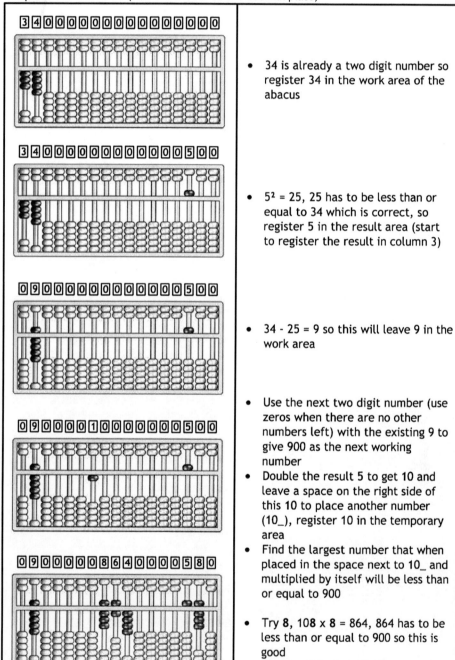

3 4 0 0 0 0 0 0 0 0 0 0 0 0 0 0 0

- 34 is already a two digit number so register 34 in the work area of the abacus

3 4 0 0 0 0 0 0 0 0 0 0 0 0 5 0 0

- 5² = 25, 25 has to be less than or equal to 34 which is correct, so register 5 in the result area (start to register the result in column 3)

0 9 0 0 0 0 0 0 0 0 0 0 0 0 5 0 0

- 34 - 25 = 9 so this will leave 9 in the work area

0 9 0 0 0 0 1 0 0 0 0 0 0 0 5 0 0

- Use the next two digit number (use zeros when there are no other numbers left) with the existing 9 to give 900 as the next working number
- Double the result 5 to get 10 and leave a space on the right side of this 10 to place another number (10_), register 10 in the temporary area
- Find the largest number that when placed in the space next to 10_ and multiplied by itself will be less than or equal to 900

0 9 0 0 0 0 0 8 6 4 0 0 0 0 5 8 0

- Try **8**, 108 x 8 = 864, 864 has to be less than or equal to 900 so this is good
- Register 8 in the result area

Figure 8.5

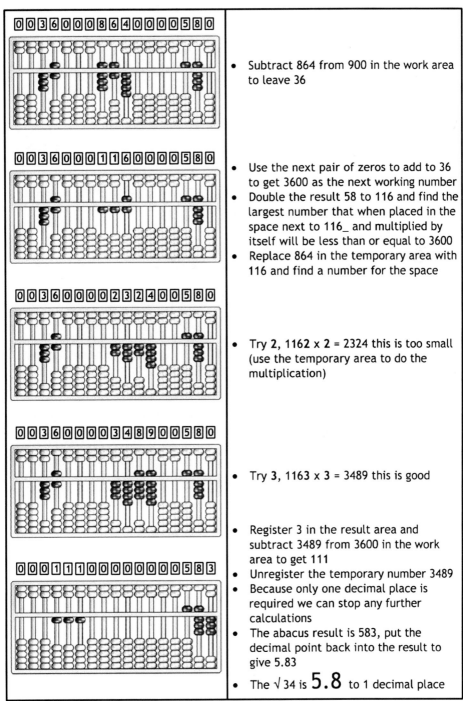

`0 0 3 6 0 0 0 8 6 4 0 0 0 0 5 8 0`

- Subtract 864 from 900 in the work area to leave 36

`0 0 3 6 0 0 0 1 1 6 0 0 0 0 5 8 0`

- Use the next pair of zeros to add to 36 to get 3600 as the next working number
- Double the result 58 to 116 and find the largest number that when placed in the space next to 116_ and multiplied by itself will be less than or equal to 3600
- Replace 864 in the temporary area with 116 and find a number for the space

`0 0 3 6 0 0 0 2 3 2 4 0 0 5 8 0`

- Try 2, 1162 x 2 = 2324 this is too small (use the temporary area to do the multiplication)

`0 0 3 6 0 0 0 3 4 8 9 0 0 5 8 0`

- Try 3, 1163 x 3 = 3489 this is good

`0 0 0 1 1 1 0 0 0 0 0 0 0 5 8 3`

- Register 3 in the result area and subtract 3489 from 3600 in the work area to get 111
- Unregister the temporary number 3489
- Because only one decimal place is required we can stop any further calculations
- The abacus result is 583, put the decimal point back into the result to give 5.83
- The √ 34 is **5.8** to 1 decimal place

Figure 8.5 (continued)

120

Example: Find the √ 12544 (no decimal places required in the answer)

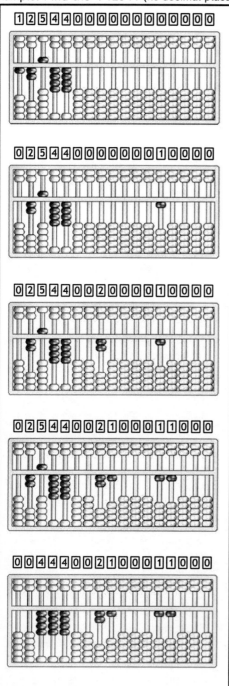

- Mentally separate the number 12544 into two digit numbers, starting at the decimal point, so 12544.0 becomes 1 25 44
- Register 12544 in the work area

- The first two digit number (in this case it is only one digit) is 1
- 1^2 = 1, register 1 in the result area (column 5) and subtract 1 from the work area (column 17)

- The next two digit number is 25, double the result 1 to get 2, register 2 in the temporary area (column 10) and remember that the next number to be found will be on its right
- Find the largest number that when placed in the space next to 2_ and then multiplied by itself will be less than or equal to 25

- Try 1, 21 x 1 = 21 (use the temporary area to register 21) which must be less than or equal to 25, therefore this is good
- Register 1 in the result area (column 4)

- Subtract 21 from 25 (columns 16 & 15) in the work area to leave 04
- Use the next two digit number 44 with the existing 4 in the work area to give the next working number as 444

Figure 8.6

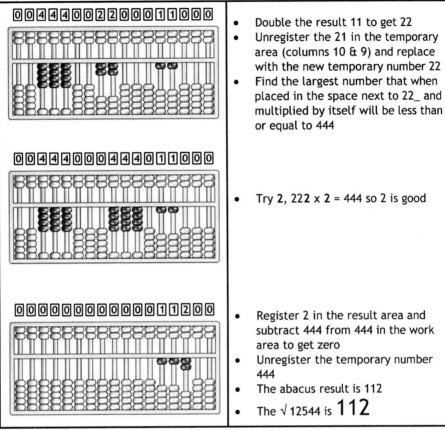

⓪⓪④④④⓪⓪②②⓪⓪⓪①①⓪⓪⓪

- Double the result 11 to get 22
- Unregister the 21 in the temporary area (columns 10 & 9) and replace with the new temporary number 22
- Find the largest number that when placed in the space next to 22_ and multiplied by itself will be less than or equal to 444

⓪⓪④④④⓪⓪⓪④④④⓪①①⓪⓪⓪

- Try 2, 222 x 2 = 444 so 2 is good

⓪⓪⓪⓪⓪⓪⓪⓪⓪⓪⓪⓪①①②⓪⓪

- Register 2 in the result area and subtract 444 from 444 in the work area to get zero
- Unregister the temporary number 444
- The abacus result is 112
- The √ 12544 is **112**

Figure 8.6 (continued)

122

 uestions | **Find the square root of the following numbers:**
(see page 142 for the answers)

Number	Question
1	√ 196 (no decimal places required in the answer)
2	√ 529 (no decimal places required in the answer)
3	√ 9216 (no decimal places required in the answer)
4	√ 26896 (no decimal places required in the answer)
5	√ 50.41 (to 1 decimal place)
6	√ 67.24 (to 1 decimal place)

PART 9

CUBE ROOTS

Cube roots 9

Finding the cube root on an abacus is similar to the method used when calculating it on paper.

Cube root

The symbol for the cube root is $^3\sqrt{}$
The root index is indicated by the number 3, showing that it is the 'cube root'. This means that we need to find a number that when multiplied by itself three times gives the number underneath the radical sign.

For example:
$^3\sqrt{64}$ means the 'cube root of 64'.
The number multiplied by itself three times to give 64 is 4 because $4 \times 4 \times 4 = 4^3 = 64$.

Number	Number to the power of 3	Cube root
1	$1^3 = 1 \times 1 \times 1 = 1$	$^3\sqrt{1} = 1$
2	$2^3 = 2 \times 2 \times 2 = 8$	$^3\sqrt{8} = 2$
3	$3^3 = 3 \times 3 \times 3 = 27$	$^3\sqrt{27} = 3$
4	$4^3 = 4 \times 4 \times 4 = 64$	$^3\sqrt{64} = 4$
5	$5^3 = 5 \times 5 \times 5 = 125$	$^3\sqrt{125} = 5$
6	$6^3 = 6 \times 6 \times 6 = 216$	$^3\sqrt{216} = 6$
7	$7^3 = 7 \times 7 \times 7 = 343$	$^3\sqrt{343} = 7$
8	$8^3 = 8 \times 8 \times 8 = 512$	$^3\sqrt{512} = 8$
9	$9^3 = 9 \times 9 \times 9 = 729$	$^3\sqrt{729} = 9$
10	$10^3 = 10 \times 10 \times 10 = 1000$	$^3\sqrt{1000} = 10$

Table 9.1

Finding the cube root of numbers can be easily done on an abacus with a little practice.

Finding the cube root of a number when calculating on paper

Example: Find the $\sqrt[3]{2197}$

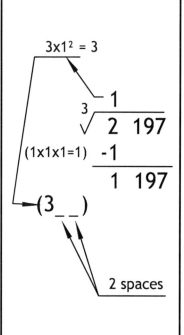

$3 \times 1^2 = 3$

$$\sqrt[3]{2\ 197} \quad \overset{1}{}$$

(1x1x1=1) **-1**

1 197

(3_ _)

2 spaces

300
+90
+9
───
399

$$\overset{1 \quad 3}{\sqrt[3]{2\ 197}}$$

-1
───
1 197

(3<u>9</u>9) -1 197
─────
0

- Separate the number 2197 into groups of three digit numbers, starting at the decimal point i.e. 2197.0 becomes 2 197 (the single digit number 2 is left over and remains alone).
- Find the largest number that when multiplied three times is less than or equal to 2 i.e. $1^3 = 1 \times 1 \times 1 = 1$
- Place this number above the number 2 and above the radical sign
- Subtract 1 (which is 1^3) from the number 2
- Bring down the next three digit number 197 and place this next to the number 1 to give a new working number of 1197
- Multiply 3 x the number above the radical sign (1) squared i.e. $3 \times 1^2 = 3 \times 1 = 3$
- Place this number 3 in brackets with two spaces on the right of it i.e. (3_ _) and place this all on the left side of the number 1197 and just below it
- We are looking for a three digit number that when multiplied by a one digit trial number is less than or equal to 1197
- Since 300 x 3 = 900 which has to be less than or equal to 1197, try number 3
- Put zeros in the spaces (3 _ _) to give 300
- Multiply 3 x the number that is above the radical sign (1), multiply by the trial number (3) then multiply by 10 i.e. 3 x 1 x 3 x 10 = 90
- Add the square of the trial number = $3^2 = 9$
- Add the numbers together to get 399 and put this number in brackets
- Multiply the number 399 by the trial number (3) to get 1197
- 1197 must be less than or equal to 1197, which it is, so number 3 is correct
- Place this number 3 above the radical sign and above the three digit number 197
- Subtract the result 1197 from the working number 1197 to leave no remainder
- The $\sqrt[3]{2197}$ is therefore **13** i.e. 13 x 13 x 13 = 13^3 = 2197

Figure 9.1

Find the $^{3}\sqrt{}$ 17576

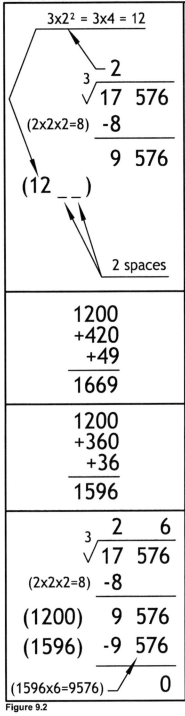

$3 \times 2^2 = 3 \times 4 = 12$

$$^{3}\sqrt{17\ 576} = 2$$

$(2 \times 2 \times 2 = 8)$ -8

$9\ 576$

$(12\ \_\ \_)$

2 spaces

1200
+420
+49
——
1669

1200
+360
+36
——
1596

$$^{3}\sqrt{17\ 576} = 2\ 6$$

$(2 \times 2 \times 2 = 8)$ -8

(1200) $9\ 576$

(1596) $-9\ 576$

$(1596 \times 6 = 9576)$ 0

- Separate the number 17576 into groups of three digit numbers, starting at the decimal point i.e. 17576.0 = 17 576
  (17 is only a two digit number as it is left over)
  The first three digit number (in this case is only two digits) is 17, find the largest number that when multiplied by itself three times is less than or equal to 17.
  So 3 x 3 x 3 = 27 which is too big
  2 x 2 x 2 = 8 which is good
- This number 2 is placed above the radical sign and the number 8 is subtracted from 17, to leave 9
- Bring down the next three digit number 576 next to the remainder 9 to give a new working number of 9576
- Calculate three times the square of the number above the radical sign i.e. $3 \times 2^2 = 3 \times 4 = 12$
- Bring this number (12) down to the left side and just below the working number 9576 and place it in brackets with two spaces on the right side of it $(12\ \_\ \_)$
- We need to find the largest four digit number that when multiplied by a one digit number will be less than or equal to 9576.
  Since 1200 x 7 = 8400 we will try the number 7
- Multiply three times the number above the radical sign (2) then multiply by the trial number (7) then multiply by 10 to get 3 x 2 x 7 x 10 = 420
- Now square the trial number to get $7^2 = 49$
- The result is 1200 + 420 + 49 = 1669
- Multiply 1669 by the trial number (7) to get 1669 x 7 = 11683, but 11683 is too large as it is not less than or equal to 9576 so we must now try the number 6 instead
- Multiply three times the number above the radical sign (2) then multiply by the trial number (6) then multiply by 10 to get 3 x 2 x 6 x 10 = 360
- Now square the trial number to get $6^2 = 36$
- The result is 1200 + 360 + 36 = 1596 which complies with being less than or equal to 9576, so the trial number 6 was correct, so place this 6 above the 576 number and above the radical sign
- Now 1596 x 6 = 9576 so subtract the result 9576 from the working number 9576 to leave no remainder

The $^{3}\sqrt{}$ 17576 is therefore 26

Figure 9.2

Finding cube roots on the abacus

It is better to use a larger abacus (with preferably more than thirteen columns) when performing cube roots. This is because the abacus is split into three areas (the same as with finding square roots).

The areas are:
    1) Work area (left side)
    2) Temporary area (middle)
    3) Result area (right side)

Decimal places

Three columns will be needed to calculate each decimal place, therefore a large abacus with more than thirteen columns would be required for calculations to many decimal places.

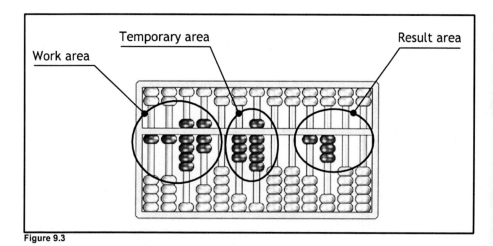

Work area   Temporary area   Result area

Figure 9.3

Example: Find the $\sqrt[3]{2197}$ (no decimal places required in the answer)

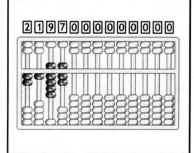

- Mentally separate the number 2197 into three digit numbers starting from the right side to get 2 197
- Register 2197 in the work area

Figure 9.4

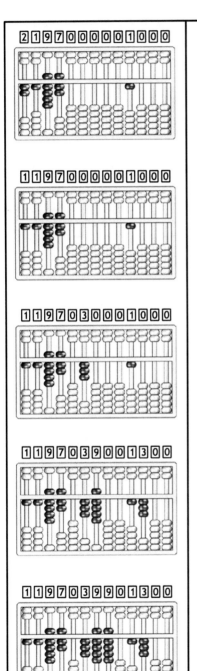

- Take the first three digit number which in this case is only one digit (as it was left over) and is the number 2
- The largest number that when multiplied three times is less than or equal to 2 is 1, because 1 x 1 x 1 = 1, register 1 in the result area (column 4)

- Subtract 1 from the first three digit number (in this case it is only the one digit number 2) in the work area, leaving 1
- The new working number is now 1197

- 3 x (first result number)^2 = 3 x 1^2 = 3, so register 3 in the temporary area (column 8)
- Since the result number is 3 we now use the next two columns to find the largest number that when multiplied by a one digit number is less than or equal to 1197, so 3_ _ is our temporary number

- Since 3 x 300 = 900 which complies with being less than or equal to 1197 the trial number will be 3
- Register the trial number 3 in the result area (column 3)
- 3 x first result number x trial number x 10 = 3 x 1 x 3 x 10 = 90
- Add 90 to our temporary number 300 to get 390

- (Trial number)^2 = 3^2 = 3 x 3 = 9
- Add 9 to our temporary number 390 to get 399

Figure 9.4 (continued)

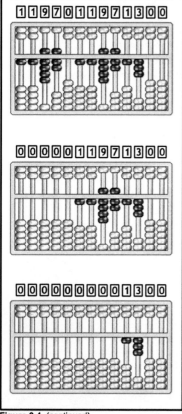

1 1 9 7 0 1 1 9 7 1 3 0 0	• Multiply our temporary number 399 by the trial number 3 to get 1197
0 0 0 0 0 1 1 9 7 1 3 0 0	• Subtract the temporary number 1197 from the working number 1197 to get all zeros
0 0 0 0 0 0 0 0 0 1 3 0 0	• Unregister the temporary number 1197 • The abacus result is 13 • The $^3\sqrt{}$ 2197 is **13**

Figure 9.4 (continued)

Finding the cube root of a decimal number using the abacus

(A seventeen column abacus will be used for the next example)

Example: Find the $^3\sqrt{}$ 85.184 (find the answer to one decimal place)

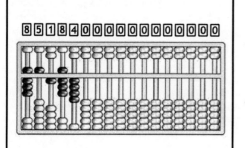

8 5 1 8 4 0 0 0 0 0 0 0 0 0 0 0 0	• Mentally separate the number 85.184 into three digit numbers starting at the decimal point to get 85 184 • Register 85184 in the work area of the abacus

Figure 9.5

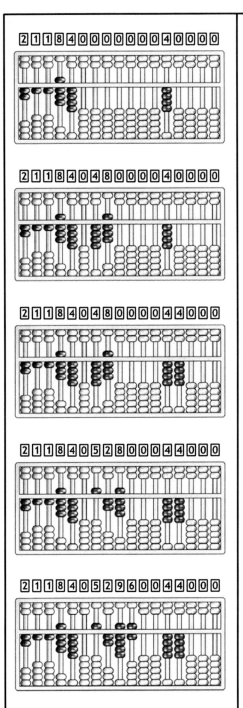

- The first three digit number (only a two digit number in this case) is 85
- The largest number that when multiplied by itself three times is less than or equal to 85 is 4 as 4 x 4 x 4 = 4^3 = 64
- Register 4 in the result area (start to register the result in column 5)

Note: As we need to calculate only to one decimal place, no extra columns will be needed.

- Subtract 64 from 85 in the work area to leave 21

- The next working number is the remainder 21_ _ _ with the next three spaces filled by the next three digit number 184 to give a working number of 21184
- 3 x (first result number)^2 = 3 x 4^2 = 3 x 16 = 48
- Register 48 in the temporary area, we now use the next two columns to find the largest number that when multiplied by a one digit number is less than or equal to 21184, so 48 _ _ is our temporary number

- Since 4800 x 4 = 19200 and complies with being less than or equal to 21184, 4 will be the trial number
- Register the trial number 4 in the result area (column 4)

- 3 x first result number x trial number x 10 = 3 x 4 x 4 x 10 = 480
- Add 480 to the temporary number 4800 to get 5280 in the temporary area

- (Trial number)^2 = 4^2 = 16
- Add 16 to the temporary number 5280 to get 5296

Figure 9.5 (continued)

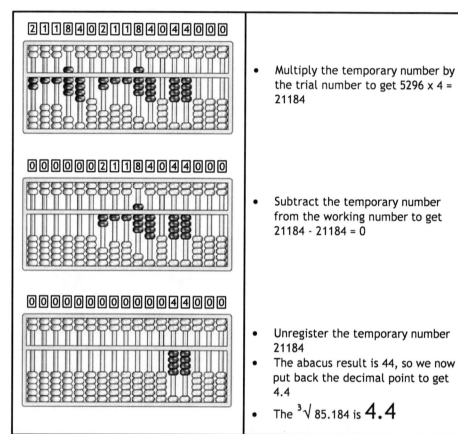

2 1 1 8 4 0 2 1 1 8 4 0 4 4 0 0 0

- Multiply the temporary number by the trial number to get 5296 x 4 = 21184

0 0 0 0 0 0 2 1 1 8 4 0 4 4 0 0 0

- Subtract the temporary number from the working number to get 21184 - 21184 = 0

0 0 0 0 0 0 0 0 0 0 0 4 4 0 0 0

- Unregister the temporary number 21184
- The abacus result is 44, so we now put back the decimal point to get 4.4
- The $\sqrt[3]{}$ 85.184 is **4.4**

Figure 9.5 (continued)

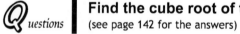

$\mathcal{Q}$uestions | ### Find the cube root of the following numbers:
(see page 142 for the answers)

Number	Question
1	$\sqrt[3]{4096}$ (no decimal places required in the answer)
2	$\sqrt[3]{12.167}$ (find the answer to one decimal place)
3	$\sqrt[3]{1728}$ (no decimal places required in the answer)

PART 10

ANSWERS

135

Answers to page 12:

Question	Answer
1	52
2	432
3	674201
4	482014365

Question	Answer
5	

Question	Answer
6	

Question	Answer
7	

Question	Answer
8	

Question	Answer
9	

Question	Answer
10	

Question	Answer
11	

Question	Answer
12	

Answers to page 30:

Question	Answer = **103**
1	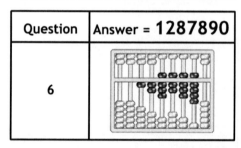

Question	Answer = **699**
2	

Question	Answer = **894**
3	

Question	Answer = **8484**
4	

Question	Answer = **66338**
5	

Question	Answer = **1287890**
6	

Question	Answer = **4326908**
7	

Question	1535 + 252 = 1787	Answer = 1787 + 22 = **1809**
8		

Answers to page 30 (continued):

Question	135254 + 2560 = 137814	137814 + 125 = 137939
9		

Answer = 137939 + 52151 = **190090**

Question	12345678 + 10000009 = 22345687
10	

Answer = 22345687 + 91255450 = **113601137**

Question	Answer = **64.511**		Question	Answer = **484.317**
11			12	

138

Answers to page 48:

Question	Answer = **57**
1	

Question	Answer = **413**
2	

Question	Answer = **806**
3	

Question	Answer = **2030**
4	

Question	Answer = **55115**
5	

Question	Answer = **389191**
6	

Question	Answer = **5207506**
7	

Question	4536 - 224 = 4312	Answer = 4312 - 12 = **4300**
8		

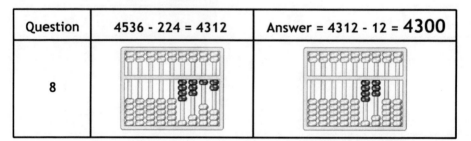

Answers to page 48 (continued):

Question	440262 - 3201 = 437061	437061 - 435 = 436626
9		

Answer = 436626 - 6713 = **429913**

Question	87654321 - 10000008 = 77654313
10	

Answer = 77654313 - 642107 = **77012206**

Question	Answer = **62.6311**
11	

Question	Answer = **14.67646**
12	

Answers to page 54:

Question	When calculating these numbers	When multiplying the following digits	Which column is your base column?
1	4321 x 3976	3 x 9	5
2	165 x 21	5 x 1	1
3	463 x 8	8 x 4	3
4	743215 x 68793	4 x 8	8
5	8176427 x 776431	6 x 6	7

Answers to page 67:

Number	Answer		Number	Answer	
1	5504		6	17.432	
2	3444		7	22.793	
3	130224		8	41679	
4	36108		9	1.296	
5	1057.5		10	337944	

Answers to page 95:

	Question	A tick is in the box containing the correct answer				
1	$\dfrac{360}{9}$	0.04 ☐	0.4 ☐	4 ☐	40 ✓	400 ☐
2	$\dfrac{392}{9.8}$	0.04 ☐	0.4 ☐	4 ☐	40 ✓	400 ☐
3	$\dfrac{207.9}{2.1}$	0.099 ☐	0.99 ☐	9.9 ☐	99 ✓	990 ☐
4	$\dfrac{46.8}{0.9}$	0.052 ☐	0.52 ☐	5.2 ☐	52 ✓	520 ☐
5	$\dfrac{0.03}{0.001}$	0.03 ☐	0.3 ☐	3 ☐	30 ✓	300 ☐
6	$\dfrac{0.0008}{0.0002}$	0.04 ☐	0.4 ☐	4 ✓	40 ☐	400 ☐
7	$\dfrac{0.8}{0.002}$	0.04 ☐	0.4 ☐	4 ☐	40 ☐	400 ✓
8	$\dfrac{0.315}{0.9}$	0.035 ☐	0.35 ✓	3.5 ☐	35 ☐	350 ☐

Number	Answer	
9	8	
10	56	
11	24	
12	43	
13	20	

Number	Answer	
14	40	
15	234	
16	66	
17	12	
18	516	

Answers to page 122:

Number	Question	Answer	
1	√ 196	14	
2	√ 529	23	
3	√ 9216	96	
4	√ 26896	164	
5	√ 50.41	7.1	
6	√ 67.24	8.2	

Answers to page 132:

Number	Question	Answer	
1	$^3\sqrt{4096}$	16	
2	$^3\sqrt{12.167}$	2.3	
3	$^3\sqrt{1728}$	12	

PART 11

INDEX

INDEX 11

CPSIA information can be obtained at www.ICGtesting.com
Printed in the USA
LVOW100103200212

269424LV00002B/196/P